LIFE'S A FISH AND THEN YOU FRY

An Alaska Seafood Cookbook

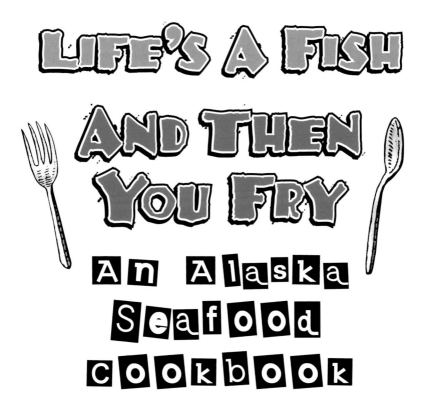

Randy Bayliss ✦ Illustrations by Ray Troll

ALASKA NORTHWEST BOOKS™

ANCHORAGE ✦ PORTLAND

An imprint of Graphic Arts Center Publishing Company
P.O. Box 10306, Portland, OR 97296-0306, 503-226-2402
www.gacpc.com

Second edition. Previously self-published in 1999 as
Fear and Poaching: Eating Southeast Alaska.

Library of Congress Cataloging-in-Publication Data

Bayliss, Randy, 1942-
  Life's a fish and then you fry : an Alaska seafood cookbook /
by Randy Bayliss ; illustrated by Ray Troll.
     p. cm.
Includes index.
  ISBN 0-88240-553-5
  1. Cookery (Fish) 2. Cookery—Alaska. 3. Cookery, International.
I. Title.
  TX747 .B349 2002
  641.6'92—dc21
                                                    2001003878

President/Publisher: Charles M. Hopkins
Associate Publisher: Douglas A. Pfeiffer
Editorial Staff: Timothy W. Frew, Ellen Harkins Wheat,
     Jean Andrews, Kathy Matthews, Jean Bond-Slaughter
Production Staff: Richard L. Owsiany, Susan Dupere
Editor: Tricia Brown
Designer: Amanda Brannon

Printed on acid- and chlorine-free paper in Singapore

Acknowledgments

Thank you, Brad Matsen, my well-fed previous editor and Strunk-meister, who taught me the meaning of clarity, brevity, and vigor, and who inspired weird culinary research for Version 1.0 of this cookbook. And thank you to Roxanne Turner, my favorite proofreader and Test Subject, who endured scorched ceilings and smoke alarms, and who hates fire and those who flambé to excess. For the art, I am beholden to Ray Troll, the Ketchikan artist who holds a black belt in Weird-Fu. Tricia Brown made editing a pleasant experience and improved the Version 2.0 product without long-term damage to our egos.

Much of this material first appeared as newspaper columns and magazine articles. My thanks to the *Alaska Fisherman's Journal*, the *National Fisherman*, *Sea Kayaker*, and the *Juneau Empire*.

And a Few Cautionary Words....

Some of the recipes portrayed in this book are based on actual events, but the amounts and proportions have been exaggerated to enhance the short-term effects of the active ingredients contained therein. Some of the names of the Test Subjects have been changed to avoid litigation.

Warning: Side Effects

The contents herein can lead to bulimia, appetite enhancement, pains in empty stomachs, insatiable cravings for unusual foods, and excessive caloric intake.

CONTENTS

CONTENTS

THE FISH ARE CALLING

I specialize in often-neglected seafoods.

INTRODUCTION
WEIRD RECIPES FOR WEIRD TIMES

Life is too short to eat bad fish.

If you're looking for a fancy cookbook with trendy designer sauces, put this one back on the shelf. I'm offended when the ill-informed call me a gourmet. Here, we're talking simple, quick, easy seafood cooking. Most of these recipes have been tested in the tiny galley of my 30-foot sailboat, often cooking underway at a 20-degree heel on a gimbaled stove, hence the pan stays on the swinging stove and the food stays in the swinging pan. As for the battered cook, well, he's just another example of the term "galley-tested."

The difference between fresh Alaska seafood and the other kind is like the difference between fresh spinach and canned spinach. Or the difference between fresh tuna and canned tuna. The cold, rich, pure coastal waters of Alaska produce seafood with bold colors, textured flesh, and healthy and tasty fats. The reason I don't use the trendy sauces is that fresh seafood cooked correctly doesn't need all those frills.

My recipes and methods focus on Alaska seafood: salmon, crab, halibut, herring, rockfish, cod, shrimp, scallops, and clams. I also specialize in often-neglected seafoods: mussels, things used as bait (squid, octopus, herring), things others throw away (salmon heads and eggs), and the ugly fish (skates, sharks, and sculpins). You'll also find recipes for seaweeds and beachside plants of coastal Alaska. There's more to Alaska than grocery-store food; you're here because of the adventure.

The more you cook seafood, the more likely you are to screw things up. I often sneak a test bite of raw seafood before buying it or after catching it. The best seafood is eaten raw (as in sushi or sashimi) or pickled (as in ceviche or Norwegian-style pickled herring and salmon). Try to leave your cooked fish moist in the middle.

My recipes are your points of departure. I urge you to substitute, change, and modify. It's your life. You make up the rules as you go along.

SECTION 1

EARTH, AIR, FIRE, AND WATER

The elements of seafood cooking include the oils, herbs, and spices found in this section. One of the main attractions for eating seafood is the health benefit. Most of these basic elements of seafood cooking have their own health benefits. Olive oil is said to remove cholesterol. Garlic is referred to as folk-remedy penicillin. Parsley cures garlic breath. Ginger cures nausea. Too healthy for you? Now you have latitude to resume some bad habits.

The following chapters describe these basic elements, their backgrounds, their health benefits, and some recipes for each.

"Extra Extra
        Superfine Virgin."
Right, you bet,
        call Ralph Nader.

CHAPTER 1
OLIVE OIL: FROM AXLES TO FRYING PANS

T he taste of olive oil marked the beginnings of civilization with the cultivation of the hardy, long-lived evergreen tree native to the Mediterranean. We will discuss the attributes and character of various olive oils, including their virginity, their uses in cooking, and several recipes highlighting olive oil with seafood.

Where vineyards flourish, so do olive trees. Like wines, olive oils have vintages and grades, good years and bad, regional varieties and flavors, and tasters and connoisseurs. Mediterranean restaurants often offer olive oil lists as well as wine lists. But whereas wines improve with age, olive oils do not.

Olive Oils as Axle Grease

Before the better-living-through-chemistry era, olive oil played more roles. The Egyptians preserved mummies with it. The Lord ordered Moses to make an oil of holy ointment from olive oil. The Romans invented a screw-press to extract olive oil. They lubricated their chariot axles with it. The Romans mixed pleasure with olive oil, also lubricating their bodies with it, saying, "Wine within and oil without." People in the remote Mediterranean still burn low-grade olive oil in lamps and use it to make soap.

Olive Oil and Heart Disease

For the people of the Mediterranean, olive oil serves as their main source of dietary fat. Butter and red meat fats do not enter their minds, much less their mouths. The people of Greece and Italy do not suffer from heart disease, even though they consume plenty of fat as olive oil.

Contrary to the "fat-free" nonsense of popular advertising, people must have fat in their diet. Fats insulate, cushion, and store fuel for the body. Some vitamins are fat-soluble only. The health problems with fats stem from eating too much fat and eating the wrong kind of fat, one of which is cholesterol. And olive oil contains no cholesterol whatsoever. Even better, dietary testing indicates that high intake of olive oil can actually lower cholesterol levels in the bloodstream.

Virginity Explained

With olive oil, the terms and labels mean different things, depending on where the olives are grown. "Virgin" olive oil from Italy differs from "virgin" olive oil from California. Other deceptive terms, like "refined" and "pure," also need explanation.

- "Pure" offers little information, meaning simply no other kind of oil is mixed with olive oil.

- "Refined" means that chemicals (solvents) were used to extract the oils from the crushed olives.

- "Hot Pressed" means high temperatures have aided removal. So more oil is yielded but it's lesser quality and has inferior taste. In the process, vitamins may be destroyed.

- "Cold Pressed" is crushed at room temperature in stone mills, and then oils are separated by gravity or by centrifuge. No chemicals are used. This high-quality type of olive oil contains vitamins E, F, and K and beta-carotenes. It also contains salicylic acid, the active agent of aspirin.

- "Filtered" can apply to any oils mentioned above. The process removes the greenish olive color and olive taste.

- "Virgin" holds various shades of meaning. In Italy, an oil of low acidity (less than 1 percent) is called "Extra Virgin." The next purest oil (up to 1.5 percent) can be called "Superfine Virgin" or sometimes "Fine Virgin." There are three other acidity grades with two names each. In the United States, it means a "first cold-pressed" oil.

- "Extra Extra Superfine Virgin." Right, you bet, call Ralph Nader.

To test the grades, place suspect oils in the refrigerator. The lower grades of oils solidify or congeal. The higher grades merely cloud up, with a few suspended crystal-like structures.

Three Kinds of Cooking Oil

A well-equipped kitchen stocks three oils, depending upon intended uses. For high-temperature frying, forget olive oil. It boils at too low a temperature to be effective. Besides, high temperatures destroy the delicate taste of olive oil, especially of the expensive oils. Use peanut oil for heavy-duty frying. For medium-duty cooking, such as sautéing onions, and low-temperature cooking, such as for eggs, use an economical clear olive oil. The Spanish oils apply excellently here. For salads and pasta and for a table condiment, use an expensive, dark green Italian oil. Don't cook with it unless you have money to burn.

Storage and Handling

Never refrigerate olive oil. If kept in a cool, dark spot, olive oil should last many months. It's better to buy small quantities. Some chefs recommend mixing butter with olive oil equally to reach a compromise between health and flavor. Since most olive oil recipes also call for garlic, store peeled garlic cloves in olive oil. The oil picks up the flavor of garlic and the garlic cloves store well, ready for other uses.

Try a simple sauce for dipping vegetables: mix freshly ground black pepper with a dash of salt in with green olive oil.

Now for some recipes.

Toast and Croutons

Ingredients:

1 loaf of quality French bread
2 cloves garlic
2 ounces olive oil
1 ounce mozzarella or Parmesan cheese, grated

For toast, slice the bread. For croutons, chop it into small cubes. Mince the garlic, and place it in a heavy skillet with the oil. Over medium (not high) heat, sauté the bread until it's crisp and brown. Toss in the cheese at the last minute. Serve croutons with soups and salads.

FISH FIGHTS!

Olive Butter

Ingredients:

4 ounces ripe olives, no pits
1 ounce green olive oil
1 ounce unsalted butter, at room temperature
1 ounce fresh basil leaves, or 2 teaspoons dried basil

Combine the ingredients in a blender or food processor, or somehow pulverize them. Serve with poached fish as follows or with sautéed chicken breasts.

Olive Oil Poached Salmon

Ingredients to serve 4:

2 pounds salmon, fillets or chunks
2 cloves garlic
2 ounces green olive oil

Chop the garlic finely and mix with oil. Massage the oil and garlic over the fish. In heavy-duty aluminum foil, wrap the fish well, folding and sealing at the top to prevent leaks. Bake at 300°F, about 10 minutes for each inch of thickness. Serve immediately with Olive Butter.

CHAPTER 2
NOBLE BASIL FLAVORS SEAFOOD ROYALLY

For centuries, basil, the "herbe royale," could only be cut by those of royal blood and only then with scythes of gold. Fortunately, in modern times the rest of us can enjoy basil, and I'll tell you how. You'll find basil fits in royally with seafood, not just king salmon, but king mackerel, king crab, and other princely fare.

Basil began its stately herb status in India, where it was worshipped. Basil's Latin name, *Ocimum sanctum*, hints at its lofty position. The common name comes from the Greek basileus, meaning "king."

Basil belongs to the mint family. The small-leafed variety growing near Genoa thrives in the dry soil, hot sun, and salty breezes of the Mediterranean. Italians complain that American basil lacks the proper pungency and tastes too minty. The Spanish grow basil to keep flies away.

Basil grows easily indoors, needing at least three hours of strong light daily and well-aerated, dry soil. The herb can be preserved by drying or, much better, by making it into pesto sauce. The pesto can be refrigerated or frozen. Chopped basil leaves can be stored immersed in olive oil for a while. The leaves can also be steamed and eaten like spinach.

Pesto Sauce

Pesto has been called the poetry of the fields, combining the fragrances of the Mediterranean. Basically, pesto uses basil, olive oil, cheese, and garlic. Purists claim that pesto must use the Italian basil grown near Genoa, which must be ground by hand in special marble mortars. Traditionalists serve pesto with fettuccine and sliced, boiled potatoes. This recipe requires a food processor instead of a mortar.

Ingredients:

2 ounces olive oil
1 cup fresh basil leaves
3 cloves garlic
1 ounce pine nuts
2 ounces Parmesan cheese

Blend all the above in a food processor. If the pesto is to be frozen, leave out the cheese until the sauce is thawed for use. Pesto can be blended into mayonnaise or incorporated as part of homemade mayonnaise. Serve Pesto Mayonnaise with poached fish and boiled potatoes.

Tomato Basil Sauce

This sauce requires no cooking and goes well with poached king mackerel. You can use Pesto Sauce (without pine nuts) as a substitute for the fresh basil, olive oil, and garlic listed below. Blend them all in a food processor or blender.

Ingredients:

1 cup tomatoes, seeds removed
4 ounces fresh basil leaves
1 ounce olive oil
2 cloves garlic

Pistou Red Snapper

Originally, "pistou" meant ground or pounded basil. With basil as the main flavoring, pistou became the name of a popular regional soup of Provence. I've modified this recipe by adding red snapper.

Ingredients for 6 servings:

1 onion
1 leek
1 ounce olive oil
4 tomatoes, divided
1 quart fish stock
1 cup French beans
1 cup lima beans
1 cup garbanzo beans
3 potatoes, chopped
2 ounces pesto
6 ounces red snapper, cut into 1-inch chunks
4 ounces spaghetti, uncooked
Croutons for garnish
2 ounces Pesto Mayonnaise
(see page 16)

Chop the onion and leek into small chunks; sauté them in the oil. When the onions become transparent, add 2 of the tomatoes, seeds removed, crushed and chopped. Add the fish stock, beans, potatoes, and pesto. Simmer for ½ hour or so. With about 10 minutes to go before the potatoes are done, add the snapper chunks. With about 4 minutes to go, add the spaghetti.

Halve the 2 remaining tomatoes, remove the seeds, and place them under the broiler until they're nearly scorched, but not black.

Serve in soup bowls, garnished with the broiled tomatoes, croutons, and a dollop of Pesto Mayonnaise.

Spinach Pesto with King Salmon

Spinach and salmon make an outstanding match, but only if you use fresh spinach. Save the canned spinach to punish misbehaving children.

Ingredients for 4 servings:

4 king salmon fillets or steaks, 6 ounces each
4 cups fresh spinach leaves, divided
1 ounce pesto
1 ounce olive oil

Broil or poach the salmon, about 10 minutes per inch of thickness. Place 1 cup of spinach leaves in a food processor; add the pesto and oil and blend. Serve salmon on beds of spinach leaves and garnish with spinach pesto.

Pesto Pasta and Scallops

Ingredients for 4 servings:

4 ounces pasta shells
2 ounces pesto, divided
1 cup white wine
1 tablespoon rice vinegar
1 pound scallops
Croutons for garnish

Boil the pasta according to instructions with an ounce of pesto. As soon as the pasta is done, drain off the boiling water. Combine the wine and vinegar, add a dash of pesto, and poach the scallops in it. Save the poaching liquid and reduce its volume by half by simmering.

In a large bowl, mix and toss the pasta, scallops, reduced poaching liquid, and remaining pesto. Refrigerate and serve with croutons.

Some folks say parsley
can be substituted
for cilantro, but they
are wrong.

CHAPTER 3

CILANTRO: ADD HEAVY METAL TASTES TO SEAFOOD

Cilantro is about as subtle as a king salmon on 8-pound test. It imparts a flat, metallic taste that reminds you of water that's run off a steam iron. Yet worldwide, cilantro ranks as the most widely used fresh herb. And for good reason. Whether you call it coriander or cilantro, both seeds and leaves make a big hit with seafood. Cilantro is especially good for shrimp and bottomfish such as cod and snapper.

Coriander belongs in the parsley family. The leaves resemble flattened parsley leaves. Some folks say parsley can be substituted for cilantro, but they are wrong; taste both for yourself and you'll find no likeness.

Coriander is one of the oldest spices known. Exodus 16:13 says, "And the House of Israel call the name Manna; and it was like coriander seed." Egyptians included the spice in the tombs of mummies in 3000 B.C. They also described its medicinal properties in the Medical Papyrus of Thebes in 1522 B.C. The seventeenth-century French used cilantro in perfumes and liqueurs.

In cooking, do not mix cilantro leaves with other spices; the cilantro is too overwhelming. Add the leaves at the end of the cooking cycle, or use them as garnish. The more finely chopped the leaves, the more pronounced the taste. Use only fresh cilantro leaves; the dried stuff doesn't compare. On the other hand, coriander seeds store well in airtight containers. The seeds have a fresh, lemonlike taste. Toast the seeds in a hot skillet, pulverize them, and add them to a seafood stew just prior to serving. Now for recipes.

Cilantro Mayonnaise

For an easy sauce for seafood, mix finely chopped cilantro leaves with store-bought mayonnaise. If you make mayonnaise from scratch, use white wine vinegar instead of lemon juice. Crush a handful of coriander seeds and let them sit in the vinegar several hours prior to use. Then add the chopped cilantro leaves while blending the mayonnaise.

This mayonnaise can be used in cooking fish. Take a large spoonful of it and massage a snapper or halibut fillet with it. Then broil, grill, or bake the fish as usual.

Cilantro Ceviche

Authentic Ceviche—a marinated raw fish or shellfish dish that's pronounced "say-VEE-chee"—uses cilantro leaves in the salsa. There are few rules on the type of seafood, but it must be fresh. The salsa can be made a week ahead of time and refrigerated. The specific ingredients vary from region to region in Mexico and Central America. Here's one version:

Ingredients for 4 appetizer-sized servings:
8 ounces snapper, fillets or pieces
Juice of 2 limes, divided

Salsa:
1 red onion
1 tomato
2 jalapeño peppers, to taste
1 green bell pepper
1 bunch cilantro
1 tablespoon olive oil

Chop the snapper into pea-sized chunks and place it in a bowl. Squeeze lime juice on it and mix well. Chill, letting it pickle for several hours. When the fish turns opaque, it's ready.

For the salsa, chop the onion, tomato, peppers, and cilantro. Mix them in a bowl, stirring in the oil and more lime juice. To serve, drain the fish and mix it with the salsa. It's especially good with tortilla chips.

Snapper Baja

Ingredients for 4 servings:

4 fillets of snapper or halibut, 8 ounces each
1 green onion, finely chopped
4 cloves garlic, mashed and chopped
1 ounce olive oil
1 ounce red wine vinegar
1 ounce white wine vinegar
1 tomato, chopped and drained
2 avocados, chopped
1 bunch cilantro; save 8 sprigs for garnish,
  the rest chopped finely

Broil or grill the snapper fillets. At the same time, start the sauce. Sauté the onions and garlic in the olive oil until the onions are soft. Add the vinegars and tomato, and let this simmer for a minute. Then toss in the avocados and chopped cilantro, and cook another minute—no more. To serve, add the sauce to the fish and garnish with cilantro sprigs.

Spicy Thai Shrimp Salad

Thai food often features cilantro. To say that Thai food is spicy means beads of sweat on your brow. This shrimp salad is milder.

Ingredients for 4 servings:

24 prawns, peeled, tails left on, sautéed in olive oil
2 red onions, both rings and chopped
1 bunch green onions, cut into 2-inch lengths
1 stalk lemon grass, minced
1 orange, peeled, in wedges
1 bunch cilantro, chopped; save 8 sprigs for garnish
1 head red leaf lettuce

Dressing:

3 ounces Thai fish sauce *(substitute by mashing an anchovy fillet in 3 ounces of water)*
3 ounces lime juice
1 teaspoon red chile flakes

Mix and toss ingredients (except lettuce leaves) with dressing. Marinate 1 hour. Place lettuce leaves on 4 chilled plates. On each plate arrange 6 prawns around the lettuce. Add salad and dressing; garnish with cilantro.

Clam Cilantro Soup

For a simple soup, try chopped cilantro with hot clam broth. The Japanese serve a beautiful, clear fish-stock soup and a single clam nestled in its shell with a sprig of cilantro in a lacquer bowl. This recipe is more basic.

Ingredients for 4 servings:

2 tomatoes, cut into wedges
24 steamed clams, shucked, with steaming liquid
    (substitute 2 cans minced clams, with liquid)
1 bunch cilantro, chopped

Simmer the tomatoes, clams, and liquid for 30 minutes. Add cilantro, simmer 2 more minutes, and serve.

Seafood Curry

In India, curry is prepared fresh for each meal. The mixture of ingredients varies from north to south and changes according to the food served. Here's a mix with your favorite seafood in mind. Add curry at the beginning of the cooking process.

Ingredients:

2 ounces coriander seeds
1 ounce cumin seeds
1 ounce fresh ginger tuber, grated
1 tablespoon turmeric powder
2 ounces coconut milk

In a hot skillet, toast the coriander and cumin seeds. Pulverize the seeds and add the remaining ingredients. Simmer this for a few minutes, and add the paste to whatever fish you're cooking.

Hara Masala

Of Indian origin, this garnish can accompany seafood. Simply chop and mix the ingredients and place them in a bowl on the table.

Ingredients:

4 ounces cilantro leaves
2 ounces mint leaves
2 ounces green chile pepper

the case of the dancing salmon

spice up your life...

CHAPTER 4
COOLING YOUR FIRES WITH SEAFOOD

Spice up your life, health, and seafood with ginger, the pungent root from the East. The Chinese regard ginger as the battery charger for the energy of life. Its medicinal properties are well known, acting to purify the body. And to promote the harmony of culinary essences, ginger balances seafood, countering the coolness of the sea with the fire of the earth.

For the weakened body and drained soul, the Chinese prescribe foods, teas, and medicines laced with ginger. Test it yourself. Chew a thick slice of a fresh ginger tuber slowly. You'll learn the meaning of "pungent," a pepperlike taste that takes control of your mouth, sending your brain a refresher lesson on taste bud capabilities. Next, your heart rate increases and beads of sweat pop out on your brow. You sense a peace coming to your digestive regions. Your inner spirits feel warmth, just as advertised.

Herbalists suggest ginger for a variety of ills. Ginger teas and ales have settled the stomach and cured nausea. Chinese sailors have chewed ginger to cure seasickness as well as to prevent scurvy. An early English cookbook prescribed ginger loaf for disturbances of the stomach. And ginger's aphrodisiac qualities have long been prescribed for those needing such help.

Ginger's purifying properties extend beyond external use. It eliminates the stench of raw flesh and accompanies wildfowl and meats to remove the odors of gaminess. For this reason, Chinese fishmongers often include slices of ginger with fish purchases to remove even the slightest odors.

In selecting fresh ginger, look for firm, unwrinkled skin. The more mature tubers of ginger are more flavorful but are also more fibrous and stringy. If you can't find fresh ginger, keep looking. Powdered ginger can be used for baking but not for seafood, although ginger juice is a good substitute if you can't find fresh. Tubers of ginger store up to a month if kept cool and dry and need not be peeled. Removing the peels is a matter of appearance. Slice ginger very thinly, cut it in strands, and then chop up the strands.

Many recipes call for the juice of ginger, and there are two ways to extract it. First, grate the tuber finely. Then, either simply squeeze the juice from your fist or pour boiling water to cover the gratings, steep for 10 minutes, and remove the pulp. Ginger juice can be refrigerated for several days.

If a recipe calls for grated ginger, do not use the standard American household grater. The proper ginger grater is a special tool more like a coarse file without holes. Use a food processor if you don't have a proper grater.

Ginger Soup

This recipe highlights the pungency of ginger. This soup started as a cold remedy but, with additions, has assumed a life of its own as a remarkable first course. I mean remarkable, too; you cannot serve this soup without getting remarks.

Ingredients for 4 servings:
8 cups fish stock *(substitute chicken stock or water)*
2 ounces finely chopped ginger
1 cup small shrimp, boiled and peeled
Juice of 2 lemons
8 healthy sprigs fresh cilantro *(substitute parsley if you have to)*

Simmer the ginger in the stock until the volume is reduced by half. Strain and discard the ginger chunks. Add the shrimp and lemon juice and simmer. Serve garnished with the cilantro. Encourage the addition of freshly ground black pepper, but warn the faint of heart to taste first.

Ginger Dipping Sauce for Steamed Crab

The Chinese consider the "coolest" of the seafoods to be crab and thus often serve crab with ginger. The following recipe best demonstrates the Oriental principle of harmony of tastes. The dipping sauce can also be served with shrimp and tempura.

Ingredients:

1 ounce grated (pulverized) ginger
2 ounces soy sauce
2 ounces rice vinegar *(substitute mild white vinegar)*
1 ounce honey
Steamed crab for 4 servings, not overcooked

Mix the sauce ingredients together and simmer for a few minutes. Cool slightly before serving with the crab.

This same ginger dipping sauce can serve as both marinade and glaze for barbecued fish. For a marinade, simply dilute the sauce with an equal amount of water. For a glaze, take a cup of the dipping sauce and simmer it in a saucepan. In a bowl, dissolve 1 ounce of cornstarch solution to the sauce until it thickens, stirring constantly. Marinate the fish for at least ½ hour. Once on the grill, brush the glaze on the fish.

DUNGENESS AND DRAGONS

Sake-Poached Mackerel

Ginger goes well with the oily fish. This recipe can also be used with bluefish and salmon.

Ingredients for 4 servings:

2 ounces finely chopped or shredded ginger
1 pint sake *(substitute dry sherry)*
1 ounce soy sauce
4 fillets of mackerel, skin left on
1 cup shredded daikon *(substitute radishes)*
2 ounces chopped green onions

Place the ginger in the bottom of a large skillet. Add the sake and soy sauce and bring to a simmer. Then set the mackerel fillets, skin side up, in the simmering sake. Place the daikon on top of the fish, and set a heavy lid on top of the daikon to press the fish down.

Poach for 10 minutes per inch of thickness of the fillet, and then carefully lift the fish out, including the daikon and ginger. Keep the fish warm while preparing the sauce by raising the heat in the skillet and reducing the volume of the poaching liquid by half. Garnish with the green onions.

TRUTH IS STRANGER THAN FISHIN'

CHAPTER 5

GARLIC AND OTHER ⭐ CURES FOR ⭐ WINTER DISEASES

You are what you eat. For example, I'm a garlic. In winter, I eat garlic to prevent and cure those nasty winter illnesses—the grippe, the hangover, the vampire. You may not want to be a garlic but yet remain healthy—there are alternatives for the socially polite. You can be a lime or even maybe a bean. What we have here, folks, are remedies, nourishing and tasty remedies, for those internal disorders of winterhood. Go ahead and pop your chemical cures, but you gotta eat, and you may as well eat those things that'd cure you anyhow.

Let's start with the No. 1 debilitator, the hangover. The standard cure is to continue drinking. That prescription can be refilled only so many times. Sooner or later, maybe April, we look for options. Look for vitamin B. I find it in miso soup, the standard Japanese breakfast that also cures seasickness and indigestion. The Japanese claim it prevents radiation sickness, relieves air pollution, and promotes long life.

The easiest miso soup is instant, now found dried in packages in most grocery stores. Add boiling water to a packet. For breakfast, poach an egg in the soup. Or add a beaten egg to boiling water for egg flower miso soup.

Later in the day, instant miso soup can be beefed up with vegetables partially stir-fried in olive or sesame oil. Japanese use leeks for special effects on colds and fevers.

Regular non-instant miso soup is easy enough to make and almost as fast as the instant. The variety of subtle supporting ingredients boggles the mind. In Japan, there are telephone recording services and calendars to suggest combinations for each day of each season. There are usually several types of miso paste available even in small specialty food stores: red, Hatcho, white, etc.

Miso Soup

The basic routine is easy: sauté lightly two ingredients in oil. Try leeks and eggs, spinach and salmon, clams and celery, onion and snapper, or mushrooms and carrots, or whatever. Don't forget that favorite classic combination of daikon and wakame. Add water and boil.

After it boils, remove from the heat. Steal ½ cup of hot broth from the pot and add 1 tablespoon of miso paste to it. Mash it up with a spoon so that the miso becomes creamy. Then pour it back into the pot. Add small amounts of pepper or parsley or curry or ginger or . . .? Officially, miso soup is served in lacquerware bowls.

Real miso soup is made with fish stock, not water. Use fish heads or packaged "dashi" stock available in your local miso store. In the absence of both, use a vegetable stock.

If nothing else, miso soup is fun to watch—the rolling protein floc reminds me of a lava lamp. And sake lovers vote unanimously for miso soup as their favorite hangover cure.

Garlic Soup

For the grippe, it's garlic soup. I've tried all kinds but this version has it all. Not just good for colds and flu, this one benefits coughs, senility, impotence, and a host of other ailments. And it enhances vitamin B uptake.

Sauté 1 cup of peeled garlic cloves and ¼ chopped onion in a jigger of olive oil until the onion is tender. Add 2 chopped tomatoes, seeds and all, and a fifth of water. Add the juice of a lime and hot pepper sauce to taste. While that boils, chop a small loaf of French bread into 1-inch cubes in a cast-iron skillet with olive oil and mashed garlic cloves. After the bread cubes brown slightly, turn the heat down low and add grated mozzarella cheese, stirring to avoid burning the cheese. Put the toasted bread and cheese in the soup bowls. Then add the soup. Save 8 garlic cloves to place between your toes—the authorized preventative for vampire bites.

Grippe Toddy

Another cold and flu remedy, by far my favorite, has side effects of relaxation of social inhibitions: the Grippe Toddy. Squeeze the juice of a lime into a mug. Add an equal amount of tequila. Fill the mug with hot water. For energy, often needed with seasickness or dehydration, add a dollop of honey. Continue to drink these until the symptoms subside or you no longer care. (Refer to paragraph 2 of this chapter in the event of overdose.) The daily tonic of lime juice boosts the body reservoir of vitamin C, constantly being drawn down in winter stress.

To control diarrhea, settle nausea, and abate seasickness, use hot chamomile tea in the Grippe Toddy. Drink chamomile tea straight during the winter disease season, again adding honey for much-needed energy and vitamin B. With upset internal organs, avoid coffee, black tea, peppers, raw fruits, greasy foods, and the like. And don't eat coconut meat.

Cover all your bets. Don't let the grippe get the upper hand. Only you can prevent intestinal inferno by eating right to keep the body up to the demands of cold stresses. You only go around once in life, and you may as well do it as a garlic.

LEVITATION AT BREAKFAST   R. T.

To eat it or
not to eat it?

CHAPTER 6

PARSLEY WORKS MAGIC WITH SEAFOOD

To eat it or not to eat it? That is the question with parsley. Should you push it around on the plate or pop it in your mouth when no one is looking? My answer is not just to eat it, but to design special recipes around it. This herb deserves more respect, and with seafood, parsley serves as more than mere ornament.

Sickly Greeks were said to be in need of parsley. For good reason, because parsley teems with vitamins C and A, calcium, and various B vitamins. Parsley cures stomach ailments, flatulence, and halitosis. It's the surest antidote to garlic breath, whether you're Greek or otherwise.

FAIRY COD MOTHER

WHEN FISHES COME TRUE

Chinese parsley has no relationship in taste to the curly-leafed or flat-leafed Italian parsley. We praised the attributes of the metallic-tasting Chinese parsley, better known as cilantro, in an earlier chapter.

The curly-leafed parsley commonly ignored on the platters of Americans and Europeans belongs to the celery family, which includes carrots, parsnips, and poison hemlock. On many beaches, a low-growing, saltwater-tolerant version abounds near its cousins, the taller beach lovages and Indian celeries. All references to parsley in these recipes mean fresh parsley, not dried.

Parsley Poaching Stock

Use this basic stock to simmer halibut or salmon. The onion, carrots, and celery can be considered optional. If you want, freeze quantities of the stock for later use, without adding the water. After poaching, save the liquid to make parsley velouté sauce in the following recipe.

Ingredients:

1 bunch parsley stems, cut in 1-inch lengths
1 handful onion skins, outer layers and other onion discards
1 handful carrot peelings
1 handful celery trimmings
1 cup white wine
2 ounces white wine vinegar
1 quart or so water

Simmer the ingredients for about a half-hour. Strain all the pulpy mass from the liquid. Immerse the fish in the simmering liquid and add boiling water if necessary to cover the fish. Poach the standard 10 minutes per inch of fish thickness.

Parsley Velouté

This recipe uses the poaching liquid from the above recipe. To substitute, use ordinary or store-bought fish stock or parsley essence, the recipe for which will be described after this. To chop parsley leaves, a food processor performs well and saves wrist soreness.

Ingredients:

1 cup poaching liquid
4 ounces parsley leaves, chopped finely
2 ounces olive oil
2 ounces flour
1 cup milk

In a saucepan, simmer the poaching liquid with the chopped parsley for less than a minute. In a medium hot skillet, add the oil and flour. Let this roux bubble for a half minute, but do not let the flour brown. Slowly add the hot poaching liquid/parsley mixture to the skillet, stirring often. Remove from the heat and add milk until the consistency seems right.

Parsley Essence

This essence amounts to a concentrated poaching liquid or sauce stock. Either freeze or keep refrigerated. When needed, merely add water and start right up.

Ingredients:

1 large bunch of parsley, stems, leaves, or both
2 cups white wine

Chop the parsley fine. Let steep in the wine for several weeks in the refrigerator. Strain the parsley and simmer the liquid until its volume is reduced by at least half.

Parsley Soup

I first encountered parsley soup in a cookbook featuring high-calcium recipes. Calcium deficiency has caught public attention in recent news about osteoporosis (brittle bone disease). This recipe adds more calcium in the form of seafoods.

Ingredients:

1 ounce olive oil
1 ounce flour
1 quart fish stock
2 cups chopped parsley
1 cup small shrimp, peeled and cooked

In a small pan, heat the oil and flour for a minute or so.
In a large soup pan, boil the stock and parsley for 10 minutes.
In a blender, mix the stock/parsley mixture in small batches, about a minute of blending per batch. Return to the pan and add the oil-flour mix, stirring constantly. Add the shrimp and heat for serving.

A great table groans
under the weight
of the feast.

CHAPTER 7
MAYONNAISE SUITS FISH TO A 'T'

A great table groans under the weight of the feast. There are bowls of boiled potatoes, platters of cold shrimp and lobster, and chilled dishes of poached salmon, cod, and halibut. Steamed artichokes and cauliflower, long loaves of French bread, and bottles of red wine surround the centerpiece—a huge bowl of the famous Mediterranean garlic mayonnaise, aioli. The crowd gathers for an afternoon of dipping seafood, sipping red wine, and licking mayonnaise off of their fingers.

Let's face it, cooked fish tastes pretty much like cooked fish. Often, sauces make the difference between an ordinary meal and a memorable feast, and mayonnaise deserves special attention in this regard. Making mayonnaise in the traditional manner is wrist work, but simple work.

Mayonnaise is egg yolks and oil, beaten together. Each egg yolk can absorb only so much oil—and only so fast. The secret is adding the oil drop by drop. Just two drops of oil added at the wrong time will ruin a batch of mayonnaise.

Olive Oil

Olive oil makes the best mayonnaise to accompany fish. Better olive oil makes better mayonnaise, so use the finest grade. The flavor of fine olive oils can vary from bland to almond to hot pepper to, of course, olive.

For the health conscious, olive oil plays well on the fish-is-heart-food bandwagon. Olive oil contains no cholesterol and has large portions of monosaturated fats. In areas where olive oil is prevalent, heart disease rates are low.

A Few Hints

All ingredients for making mayonnaise should be at room temperature before you start. The mixing bowl should be rinsed with warm water and dried out. Be sure to measure the oil carefully so that not too much is added.

The egg-oil mixture can be beaten using a whisk or a mortar and pestle; a hand-cranked eggbeater; or an electric eggbeater, blender, or food processor. If you're beating by hand, seek assistance for adding the drops of oil. And once you start adding oil, don't stop until the mayonnaise has thickened.

Basic Mayonnaise

Figure out how much mayonnaise you want (1 egg yolk makes almost a cup). Add the egg yolk(s) to a bowl and beat for 5 seconds if using an electric device such as a blender; continue for a total of 1 minute if beating by hand. For each egg yolk, beat in a dab of prepared mustard and a teaspoon of something sour: a good wine vinegar, fresh lime juice, or lemon juice.

Measure out your olive oil, using a minimum of ½ cup—and never more than a cup—per egg yolk. Add a drop of olive oil to the egg yolk/vinegar mixture and beat it in. When the first drop disappears, add another drop. At that point, while still beating, you can add the rest of the oil a bit faster, maybe in a fine stream. When the mayonnaise thickens, stop beating. Never add oil so fast that puddles build up. Once it's finished, keep the mayonnaise refrigerated.

If your mayonnaise later separates and puddles of oil appear, it has "turned." To save it, place 1 tablespoon of prepared mustard in a bowl and mix in an equal amount of mayonnaise. Then, spoonful by spoonful, mix in more mayonnaise.

Aioli, or Garlic Mayonnaise

For each cup of mayonnaise, pulverize or blend about 4 peeled garlic cloves to produce garlic paste. Add this paste to the egg yolks before they're beaten in the first step of the Basic Mayonnaise recipe, and proceed as before.

Mayonnaise Verde

This green mayonnaise enhances most seafood nicely, but with poached salmon, it's spectacular. For each cup of mayonnaise, shred about 4 spinach leaves, a few watercress leaves (if available), and a couple of parsley sprigs, free of stems. Place the greens in a bowl and pour boiling water over them.

Let them steep for a few minutes, then squeeze the water out of the limp greens and blend them into a paste. Mix the paste in with the egg yolks in the first step of the Basic Mayonnaise recipe, and proceed as before.

Mayonnaise aux Fines Herbes

Various other herbs can be pulverized and mixed into the Basic Mayonnaise recipe. A dill-based mayonnaise would accompany Scandinavian-type fish: salmon, cod, and maybe halibut. A basil mayonnaise sounds good with Italian-style snapper. Try a cilantro and cayenne pepper mayonnaise with Caribbean fish. Serve tarragon mayonnaise with sole, using a tarragon vinegar in the recipe.

Quick-and-Dirty Mayonnaise

Use a good-quality store-bought mayonnaise, or substitute yogurt or sour cream. You might consider enriching the off-the-shelf product by beating in an extra egg yolk, a tablespoon of olive oil, and a dab of mustard.

To make quick aioli, look for garlic paste in supermarkets or delicatessens; much superior to garlic powder, it often comes in toothpaste-type tubes. Even better is making up a batch of your own garlic paste ahead of time for future use.

Garlic Paste

Peel the cloves from a couple of garlic bulbs and blend them in a food processor or blender. Mix in a small amount of olive oil to increase the shelf life of the paste, which should be kept tightly sealed and refrigerated. For the other spiced mayonnaises, dried spices can, of course, be substituted for fresh ones.

But you'll find that homemade mayonnaise, especially the garlic variety, will change your outlook on seafood cooking.

Tricks of the Trade — A Seafood Mayonnaise Recipe

You can try this recipe in your very own kitchen, but, with encroaching governmental control over our fun and our privacy, I don't know how much longer it will be legal.

Lay out a sheet of heavy plastic to catch any fallout. Stand on the plastic sheet. In one hand, take a large chunk of halibut. With the other hand, reach deeply into a large jar of aioli and take a large handful. With closed eyes, gently caress and rub the aioli into the fish flesh. Be thorough and take your time. Then bake the halibut at 350°F for 20 minutes.

Try it. Your feelings about mayonnaise will never be the same.

"THE FRY"

SECTION 2
MY FAVORITE COOKING METHODS

You can ruin any good seafood with careless cooking methods. I like to stress poaching, because it's forgiving and you can make such good vegetables and basic sauces using the poaching liquors. Grilling and flambéing are two other favorites.

The most common mistake in fish cooking is overcooking. Start with the "ten minutes per inch" rule for cooking time. Test the fish frequently with a knife to see how the insides look, and get the fish off the fire while the flesh is still moist. I like to see my fish look almost raw in the center. If your guests like it more done, that's what the microwave is for.

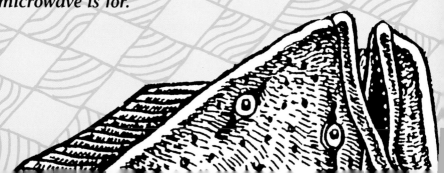

Real men don't
poach fish.

CHAPTER 8

POACHING: YOU'LL NEVER FRY AGAIN

R eal Men don't poach fish. They fry it. Or bake it. One way or another, Real Men usually screw it up. Delicate and misunderstood, more fish has been ruined by bad cooks than has been pirated by illegal foreign processor ships in the 200-Mile Zone. But by the time you've finished this section on poaching, you'll never fry again.

The original sin of fish abuse—overcooking—results in dry, flavorless pulp. Poaching fish makes it far more difficult to overcook. For one thing, the temperature of poaching is less than that of other cooking methods. For another, tasty juices are less apt to be driven off when the fish is immersed in the poaching liquor. And if you follow one simple commandment, and other commonsense doctrine herein, you'll never overpoach. But first, let's talk liquor.

Court Bouillon

Poaching liquor, or, for the more refined, "court bouillon," never comes out the same. You can fix large batches, and quickly. Leftovers can (and should) be easily frozen. Then the spices and oils continuously cohabitate, and there's no delay in thawing it when you need poaching liquor in an emergency.

Begin with a bottle of dry, white wine. Chablis is great. Drink half and dump the other half in a huge cauldron. Throw in an equal amount of fancy vinegar, maybe with tarragon leaves right in the bottle. Start this mixture boiling. Now, with creative style, add chopped vegetables and spices of your choice: onion, celery, parsley, whole peppercorns, allspice, bay leaf, thyme, cloves, and whatever else you like or think you might like. I've researched libraries of the great culinary universities, Old World and New, for the secret of the proper spice mixtures. Don't be intimidated. There is no "proper" mix—it's all yours to develop for yourself. For the timid among you, I'll offer sample combinations to start with.

This variety of spices is one of two reasons that poaching is never the same. Be reckless. Abandon your inhibitions. But keep records of your spice mixes and ratings—refining your spice mixes can be highly scientific.

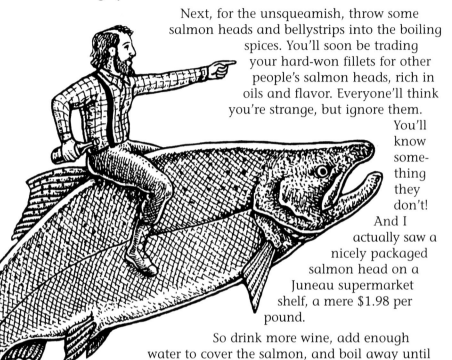

Next, for the unsqueamish, throw some salmon heads and bellystrips into the boiling spices. You'll soon be trading your hard-won fillets for other people's salmon heads, rich in oils and flavor. Everyone'll think you're strange, but ignore them. You'll know something they don't! And I actually saw a nicely packaged salmon head on a Juneau supermarket shelf, a mere $1.98 per pound.

So drink more wine, add enough water to cover the salmon, and boil away until the meat falls off the head. You'll find an amazing amount of rich meat there, and don't forget the cheeks. Throw away all the grisly parts. Cover the pot. Don't let anyone look at the heads.

Now drink some more wine and taste this poaching liquor, or court bouillon (what an elegant name, only proper for fine fish). Adjust spices, pH, and add more wine. Taste it again. Make it better. With this liquor we poach, impregnating the unique spice flavors into delicately cooking fish and accompanying vegetables. And with this liquor we also make sauces. Some folks just can't wait and are compelled to guzzle the poaching liquor straight up, with hot garlic bread and wine chasers.

Most poaching recipes mention cheesecloth. I never use the stuff. It sounds too much like doing laundry. All you want is to keep the fish from falling apart. It's easier to leave the skin on or bones in.

Now for the Basic Commandment:

> # Thou Shalt Boil Fish
> # 10 Minutes per Inch of
> # Fish Thickness

So if the average body thickness of your fish or fillet is 2½ inches, the boiling time is 25 minutes. Time it. Don't boil it one second longer. Take the fish out right away. Test the fish by parting the flesh, which should flake easily. It should be moist and almost uncooked, as in the rarest of T-bone steaks. If it's not quite done, boil the fish for another minute and test it again. That's all there is to it. The only excuse for overcooking is sinful negligence.

Boiling fish 10 minutes per inch may not be as easy as it sounds. To maintain consistency, follow these rules.

1. Use lots of poaching liquor in a large pot.

2. The liquor should be boiling rapidly before the fish is added. Both of these cut down on the time needed to get the liquor back up to boiling temperature after the addition of cold fish. After boiling temperatures are reached again, cut down the heat to a simmer.

3. Try to use fish that has been cut into pieces of uniform thickness; or throw smaller chunks into the boiling liquor later on in the cooking cycle. The idea here, of course, is to avoid overcooking the small pieces.

You'll recall that the variety of spices in the poaching liquor was one of two reasons that poached fish never tastes the same twice. Now for the second reason: at this stage feel free to add your favorite vegetable(s) to the boiling liquor. Potatoes, tomatoes, onions, celery, Brussels sprouts, broccoli, spinach, peas, cauliflower—anything and everything you like. Some of these may take longer to cook than the "10 minutes per inch" rule, so add them earlier. The flavors of the vegetables mix with those of the spices, adding to the taste of the fish.

So don't violate the Commandment of 10-minutes-per-inch and thou canst not sin by overpoaching. But there remains the sin of burning the sauce, so keep the faith and read on, for a second Commandment awaiteth:

Thou Shalt Not Burn Thy Sauce

Don't kid yourself. If you cook fish, it tastes like fish. The secret to delicious fish, though, is the delicious sauce you put on it. Perhaps you've thought this was a chapter on how to poach fish. Wrong. The objective all along was the SAUCE.

Recall what's been done up to now. First, wine and spices were comingled with fish oils to create the poaching liquor. Then vegetables and the fish itself were poached in same, extracting more flavors into the liquor. If you've followed our advice, you may have even frozen and recycled the poaching liquor and inherited twice the flavors. Now, we make the Sauce from the poaching liquor with its rich wealth of oils, juices, tastes, spices, and, of course, whatever wine you didn't drink. My God, man, throw away the fish and savor the sauce.

There's no secret to not burning sauces: just never turn the stove on "high." Use "medium" and patience.

And there's no secret to making sauces. Standard Government Issue: use equal amounts of butter and flour. Melt the butter first, add the flour second. Let it bubble for a minute or two. Don't let it get too brown, but cook it long enough to rid yourself of the raw flour taste. (Or see the Cajun Roux recipe below.) Add small batches of poaching liquor while it's still hot and throw in some wine, a little bit at a time until you like the looks of it. Add milk or cream or sour cream if you feel compelled to. For each ounce of butter-flour roux, you'll use about a cup of liquid. Taste it. Add more wine and spices if needed. Taste it again.

You've just made the Sauce. Not just any sauce but The Sauce because of its poached heritage!

Of course, since there are variations on a theme of ordinary sauces, you have an opportunity to mess up The Sauce. Don't waste the time. By now the fish and vegetables are cooling off because you've forgotten to put them in a warm spot—which is just as well because you wouldn't want to overcook the fish. Have confidence. Go ahead and dump The Sauce on the fish and vegetables without asking guests if they want it. Some unknowing fool might refuse.

Here's another sauce deviation that's worth trying. Use premade Cajun Roux instead of the butter-and-flour base mentioned above. The Cajun Roux adds flavor.

Cajun Roux

This roux is only for those without attention deficit disorders. Set up a stool near the stove, get a beer and a book or good music. Mix equal parts of butter and flour in a skillet over medium to low heat. With a wire whisk, stir constantly until it turns light shoe-leather brown. Not dark brown. It must take more than 15 minutes but less than an hour. The browned flour imparts a distinctive, slightly burnt taste. You can store roux in a refrigerator or freezer for a long time.

Once you've matched the simplicity of poaching with the imagination of off-breed fish, ingredients, and spices, you'll become an expert fish cooker for life. You can poach seven days a week, and it'll never be the same.

Neither will you.

The Hemingway heroes
loved to fish,
and they loved to eat
their catch.

CHAPTER 9

COOKERY À LA HEMINGWAY: PAN FRY TO STIR FRY

The Hemingway heroes loved to fish, and they loved to eat their catch. As both Hemingway and his heroes matured, so did their tastes in fish cookery. For example, Nick Adams, a character in the early short stories, fried trout in a cast-iron skillet with bacon grease over a streamside fire. Then, in Hemingway's Paris-based writings, done between the great wars, reference is made to Trout au Bleu, served with a dearly bought white burgundy. And the Thomas Hudson characters of the later Caribbean period grilled their dorado steaks over charcoal, with gin and tonic on the side.

Trout American

In his own early wild-and-reckless days, Hemingway cooked his trout American-style. After administering a sharp rap on the fish's head, he slit the trout from vent to the tip of the jaw. The insides and tongue came out cleanly and were left for the morning's mink patrol. Then, after setting his folding grill over a streamside fire, Hemingway would scrape a lump of bacon grease from a can and slide it, sputtering, across a black iron skillet large enough to hold the trout, head to tail. He'd roll the trout in cornmeal and carefully place them in the skillet.

After the trout browned, Hemingway turned them carefully, layering strips of soft-cooked bacon on the crisp side to baste the fish. He decanted coffee from a pot on the grill and, using forked branches, lifted the trout from the skillet to the plate on his knees. And the trout were true and good—and loaded with cholesterol.

That was 1919 on the banks of the Black River in the Pine Barrens. Four years later, Hemingway found his Moveable Feast in Paris, where his tastes adapted to fine European fish cooking: No more bacon grease. Hemingway now feasted on Trout au Bleu.

Trout Parisian

As before, the trout were fresh; the killing and cleaning were the first steps in the recipe. The cleaned trout were sprinkled with wine and vinegar and plunged into a court bouillon containing extra doses of vinegar. After being boiled for 8 minutes or so, the trout were drained, garnished with parsley, and served with melted butter or hollandaise sauce. Trout au Bleu can be served cold, warm, or hot.

About court bouillon: a version of this fish-cooking stock can be made quickly as follows: Mix together equal amounts of clam juice, white wine, and water. Add thin slices of onion and parsley stems. Simmer for a few minutes.

As a side dish in Paris, Hemingway enjoyed boiled potatoes with olive oil and freshly ground black pepper. When he could afford it, he also relished boiled leeks with a vinaigrette made from olive oil, white wine vinegar, and freshly ground black pepper.

Scampi Brochette

Hemingway's European travels took him back to Italy, where he was wounded during World War I. There, he discovered a favorite prawn dish: Scampi Brochette. In several writings, he likens their antennae to the mustaches of Japanese admirals.

For the brochette, peel and devein the prawns. Place the prawns in a bowl with a mixture of equal parts of olive oil and vegetable oil. Add bread crumbs and mix with the oil until the prawns show a light, creamy coating. Now add chopped garlic, parsley, and freshly ground black pepper, and marinate for half an hour at room temperature.

Preheat your broiler at its maximum setting. Take several flat-edged skewers and impale the breaded prawns, curling them tightly so the skewer pierces the body at least at three points. Broil for no more than 4 minutes on a side. The prawns are done when they show a brown crust. Serve with lemon wedges and garnish with parsley.

LIFE IS BUT A STREAM

Chinese Shrimp

Hemingway toured China briefly, but even that brief exposure to Chinese food dramatically influenced his eating habits. He pronounced a stir-fried-shrimp dish "the best meal I have ever eaten in my life."

Ingredients:

1 cup bean sprouts
1 small red onion, chopped
1 cup diagonally sliced celery stalks
1 8-ounce can mushrooms, either straw or shiitake
1 pound prawns, shelled and deveined
1 can fried noodles

Using peanut oil in a large skillet at high heat, quickly sauté the vegetables, shrimp, and noodles. When done, the celery should hardly be cooked. Serve atop white rice and have several Asian sauces available at the table.

Snapper Stew

Hemingway's deep-sea fishing centered on his boat, the *Pilar*. The boat's master and cook, Gregorio Fuentes, became well known for his Snapper Stew, highly acclaimed by Hemingway's many famous fishing guests. This calls for one red snapper, whole, without guts, but you can substitute rockfish or bass.

Sauce Ingredients:

1 Bermuda onion, chopped
1 red bell pepper, chopped
6 cloves garlic, more if you can take it
Olive oil
1 8-ounce can tomato puree
1 bay leaf
1 tablespoon dried Mexican oregano
1 4-ounce can green olives with pimentos, chopped
½ glass of sherry (you know what to do with the other half)
1 ounce capers
1 ounce raisins

An hour before beginning to cook, take a red snapper and score it several times, cutting diagonally to the backbone. Rub salt into the cuts.

Select a pan large enough to hold the snapper, head and tail. In it, first make the sauce. Sauté the onion, pepper, and garlic—use plenty of garlic—in olive oil, until the onion turns slightly soft. Add a can of tomato puree, a bay leaf, and oregano. Let this simmer for half an hour. Then add the rest of the ingredients. Simmer for a few minutes more.

Scrape the salt off the snapper, rinse it slightly, and place it into the simmering sauce. Cook slowly until the snapper turns white and the flesh firms up. Serve, with sauce, over white rice.

Hemingway's cooking tastes may have matured from bacon grease to olive oil, but he always relished "good, fresh fish." In his later years, his health failed him. A careful diet that included grilled fish helped him control the weight and blood-pressure problems.

CHAPTER 10

GRILLING:
OUT OF THE
FRYING PAN,
ONTO THE
BARBECUE

Throw a hunk of seafood on a fire and enjoy it the way we used to in the good old prehistoric days. There's something pleasingly primitive about barbecued fish. Growl when you eat it. I spoiled myself with a rail-mounted barbecue grill on my boat, and there was a lot of growling around the boat harbor that summer.

The aromas of spring and charcoal-broiled king salmon belong together. If you don't have a barbecue grill on your boat, get one—they're fantastic.

As with all fish, barbecued fish must not be overcooked. Stick with the "10 minutes per inch of thickness" rule and flip the fish over halfway through the cooking time. The essence of alder smoke adds magic to the grilled fish flavors.

And let us not ignore the virtues of charcoal-grilled clams and oysters. Simply lay them on the grill and once open, dip them in melted butter and dredge them in a mixture of Parmesan cheese and celery seed. The juices steam when they hit the coals and contribute to the enjoyment.

There are some who say the worst thing about writing oyster recipes is that oysters are best raw. Maybe so, but I hate to shuck oysters, so smoked oysters make a tasty compromise.

Skewered Scallops

No compromises with skewered scallops though. These are the best. On a wire or bamboo skewer, weave strips of bacon back and forth as scallops are threaded on. Some people alternate water chestnuts, mushrooms, and the like, but that just takes up valuable space for scallops—you'll find that a bad habit. But if anyone knows of better scallop treatment, call me collect.

Fish Kabobs

Another skewered recipe is fish kabobs. Two variations come to mind. First would be to alternate prawn-sized shrimp with chunks of pineapple or sections of oranges. Grill them with the shells intact. Onions, bell pepper, cherry tomatoes, and the like can be substituted in the basic shrimp-pineapple routine, but they, too, are a waste of valuable skewer space.

The second variation calls for a firm white fish—halibut, sablefish, shark—alternating with onions or leek chunks. For this, I'd suggest a teriyaki sauce. Baste fish generously and often. On this variation, feel free to skewer any substitutions you like. It's all good teriyaki-style.

Teriyaki Sauce

Ingredients:

1 cup soy sauce
1 cup sake
1 cup mirin
2 ounces rice vinegar
2 tablespoons cornstarch

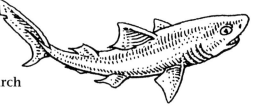

Add ingredients to a saucepan, bring to a boil, and add cornstarch to thicken.

Sweet & Sour Sauce

Ingredients:

1 cup crushed pineapple
4 ounces sake
3 tablespoons miso
3 tablespoons rice vinegar
2 tablespoons ketchup
1 tablespoon honey
1 teaspoon fresh grated ginger root
1 tablespoon of cornstarch

Sweet and sour prawns grill well. The sauce is simple: bring ingredients to a boil, and add cornstarch to thicken. Heap this sauce onto the shrimp as it's grilling.

Juneau Salmon Bake BBQ Sauce

The Juneau Salmon Bake Barbecue Sauce remains my favorite. And it's as simple as it is excellent. Add a cup of brown sugar to a melted stick of butter and the juice of half a lemon. Dredge the salmon fillets in oil before putting them on the grill, skin side down at first. Baste both sides, turning frequently. You'll use this one a lot.

Mexican-Style Sauce

For halibut steaks headed for the grill, two sauces are suggested. First, a Mexican-Style Sauce that also goes well with swordfish steaks. In ½ cup of olive oil, sauté a chopped onion, 5 to 7 crushed cloves of garlic, chopped green onions, a couple chopped jalapeño peppers, and chopped fresh cilantro (substitute parsley). Sauté until the onions start to become transparent, then add 2 or 3 chopped tomatoes. Baste the fish with this sauce while on the grill.

Ginger Sauce

The second sauce is a simpler ginger sauce. Grate fresh ginger and add to soy sauce. Thicken with cornstarch. Both marinate and baste the grilled fish with this sauce.

Asian Sauces

Two Japanese-style fish barbecue recipes should be tried. The first uses a simmered miso basting sauce. Add a jigger of mirin, 2 tablespoons of sake, and an egg yolk to 1 cup of sweet white miso. For variations, add sesame seeds or grated ginger. Bring this mixture to boiling and simmer for a few minutes. Chunks of salmon, or whatever, should be skewered, perhaps alternating with parboiled leek chunks, and broiled for about 10 minutes. After the fish is mostly broiled, only then is the basting sauce added. Return to the grill for a final minute or so.

The second miso method simply involves spreading the miso— red, barley, or sweet white—directly on the fish steaks and refrigerating them for one or two days to "pickle" the fish. Scrape most of the miso off and go for the grill. *Hai, zehi doozo.*

With most fish recipes, it's the sauce that really makes the final difference. But with the barbecue, the grilling and alder smoke enhance both the taste of the fish and the taste of the sauce. The old ways are sometimes better, and cooking over an open fire is pretty old.

Good grilling and good growling.

HOWLING DOGS

Some people will
smoke anything.

CHAPTER 11

SMOKING: ALL SMOKE, NO BUTTS

Some people will smoke anything. These days, you can find smoked salmon, steelhead, halibut, sablefish, albacore, and even eulachon (also known as "hooligan") on many grocery store and smoked-fish-specialty-shop shelves. How nice it is to see top-quality smoked fish being processed and marketed throughout the state. Visiting sport fishermen can get their daily catch smoked and vacuum-packed while they wait, 24-hour turnaround, and forget about schlepping ice chests through the airport.

Smoked salmon has always been a treat, with a cold beer chaser. This chapter deals with how to cook and eat smoked fish, not how to smoke them.

Generally, smoked fish excel when accompanied with cream sauces or with potatoes or eggs. Both quiches and soufflés accept smoked salmon or sablefish with contentment. Smoked fish accentuates pasta dishes—I keep packages of smoked salmon and spinach fettuccine aboard my boat for emergency gourmet meals, just in case the crew doesn't haul in fresh fish for the evening feed. When experimenting, think of smoked fish as a substitute in recipes calling for ham or bacon.

Now for some specific breakfast, salad, and entree dishes.

Lox and Eggs

Chop a red onion, a green bell pepper, and a few mushrooms, and sauté them lightly in butter, at medium heat. Don't overcook—the onion slices should be crisp, not limp. Then add some sliced lox or shredded smoked salmon. Beat half a dozen eggs with a couple of jiggers of cream and slowly add it into the salmon/vegetable mixture. Cook over very low heat, stirring slowly and continuously. Serve over toast or with bagels and cream cheese.

S.O.S.: Salmon on a Shingle

This dish feeds huge quantities of folks for breakfast. Make mass amounts of white sauce, using these proportions: 2 tablespoons of butter melted in a saucepan. Add and heat (but don't quite brown) 2 tablespoons of white flour. Slowly add, stirring often, a cup or so of cream (substitute half-and-half) until the sauce looks thin enough. Add shredded smoked salmon, chopped hard-boiled eggs, and parsley. For variety, throw in a can of peas. Serve over toast or in a bowl with croutons.

Salmon Pasta Salad

Mix dill, chopped shallots, mayonnaise and yogurt, and flaked smoked salmon with cooked and chilled pasta shells. Grated cheese optional.

Salmon Pancakes

Simply mix some shredded smoked salmon into the pancake batter and proceed normally. Make a cream sauce, add more shredded smoked salmon, and serve the sauce on top of the pancakes. For the upwardly mobile, make the batter very thin, add grated cheese and a dash of sherry to the sauce, and pretend you're into crepes.

Salmon Potato Salad

Slice red potatoes, boil them until crunchy, and cool them. Add chopped celery, radishes, and green and red onions. Mix in equal volumes of mayonnaise and plain yogurt. Also add flaked smoked salmon. Spice with mustard and dill. Garnish with capers, chopped egg, and so forth. Lemon juice or vinegar will add some zing.

Smoked Salmon Nicoise

This recipe can be fancy, but it sure hits the spot. Toss up chunks of smoked salmon, tomato wedges, chopped endive (or lettuce), olives, hard-boiled eggs, artichoke hearts, asparagus spears, green beans, capers, anchovies, green onions, and cooled pasta shells. Prepare a dressing by blending olive oil, dijon mustard, lemon juice, minced garlic cloves, freshly chopped basil (or pesto), chopped parsley, mashed anchovies, a few capers, and freshly ground white (or black) pepper.

Sablefish à la Candia

Thanks to the fine people at Juneau's Silver Lining Seafood store for this inspiration. Slice up several red potatoes and line the bottom of a baking dish with the slices. Then add a layer of flaked smoked sablefish. The third layer should be some sort of green vegetable, such as broccoli, bell pepper, or the like. Then repeat the sequence until you run out of ingredients or baking dish freeboard. Add a cream sauce, maybe with nutmeg. Bake until the potatoes are crunchy.

Eggs and Salmon, Scandinavian-Style

Thinly slice smoked salmon and place the slices on top of warmed pumpernickel bread. Add poached eggs and freshly chopped dill (substitute dill seed if there's no fresh dill about).

Smoked Salmon Fettuccine

Finely chop a few shallots (substitute green onions) and sauté them slightly in olive oil. Add shredded smoked salmon, a splash of Scotch whiskey, and a cup or so of cream. Let this thicken and pour over a platter of hot spinach fettuccine. As options, stir in grated cheese and freshly chopped basil. Reduce the amount of cream and let the fettuccine cool, and this recipe makes for a superb cooled pasta salad.

Finnan Sablefish

Sablefish resembles smoked haddock enough to use it as a substitute in Finnan Haddie recipes. Poach the sablefish in milk or cream and use the juices to make a cream sauce. Serve with chopped egg or parsley garnish. Add mustard, sautéed onion, and mushrooms to spice up the sauce. Serve it neat, or over noodles or rice.

Salmon-Stuffed Potatoes

Bake potatoes normally, slice them in half, and scoop out the insides, leaving a potato shell for stuffing. Mash the scooped-out potato innards, adding butter, sour cream, finely chopped chives or green onions, and finely shredded smoked salmon. Spoon this mixture back into the potato shells, reheat, and serve.

Scotch-Flavored Smoked Salmon

Make a heavy cream sauce and let it simmer for a while to thicken up even more. Add a pad of butter and splash of Scotch whiskey. Throw in some shredded smoked salmon and serve over hot noodles.

Sablefish Cakes

Mix up equal portions of mashed potatoes and finely flaked smoked sablefish, add a small batch of minced ginger and a beaten egg or two. Form small patties and sauté them slowly in butter.

Smoked Salmon and Potatoes

Another rapido meal, great for breakfast or later. Quarter unpeeled potatoes and boil them for 10 minutes or so. Quartered onions may be added, depending upon the mood of the crowd. Add chunked smoked salmon in sufficient time to warm them up, drain the boiling water, and add butter and chopped parsley.

Smoked salmon tastes wonderful by itself, so it makes sense that smoked salmon used in recipes tastes even better. The same can be said of the other smoked fish. With the right combinations and accompaniments, this certainly rings true.

Sablefish and Split Pea Soup

Think of smoked sablefish as a substitute for ham in split pea soup. It works fine. If you use the various packaged instant or near-instant pea soup mixes, just add in the shredded smoked sablefish. Starting from scratch with dried split peas, be sure to consider plenty of sautéed onion, carrots, curry spices, garlic, and so forth. This soup stands out in those crisp winter days, a cure for hypothermia and source for cold-weather energy supply.

CHAPTER 12
PICKLING: HOT SAND AND SEAFOOD

Are you getting hyped for your winter vacation in the sun? Before you go, expose yourself to sunlamps. And expose yourself to grand Mexican and Hawaiian food. Forget about tacos and buried pigs; seafood makes the superior Mexican and Hawaiian fare. The following recipes zing with tart, spicy freshness that's best accompanied by cold beer and hot sand.

First get in the proper vacation mood. Start the morning practice with Gazpacho Mary. Into your blender, dump 1 cup of vodka, 1 cup of tomato juice, 3 tomatoes, an onion, a cucumber, a green pepper (seeds removed), and the juice of a lemon. Add spices to suit your taste. Choose between chopped chile peppers, horseradish, Tabasco, scallions, parsley, Worcestershire, celery seed, and the like. Serve it ice cold. If it doesn't taste quite correct, finish it off, and get it right the next time. For a surprising variation, blend in a big handful of shrimp from Petersburg, Alaska.

Now that you've had a proper breakfast, it's time for the mid-day marinated seafood salads. Here are three for tropical conditioning.

Midday heat in Mexico calls for Ceviche, a spicy marinated salad with pickled seafood. Ceviche tradition would suggest a light, firm white seafood, normally something like scallops. An Alaska favorite would be halibut. I prefer calamari by far. Rich, oily fish such as black cod or red fish such as salmon work almost as well.

You may not substitute for two of the ingredients in Ceviche: first, you must squeeze juice from real limes or lemons; the bottled juice will not do. Second, you must use cilantro, a.k.a. coriander leaf. If you ever see fresh cilantro in your produce section, buy and freeze it for the next time you make Ceviche. Some people say parsley can be used in place of cilantro, but they are liars.

Ceviche

Ingredients:

1 tomato
2 scallions
1 small green bell pepper
1 lime, peeled
1-2 green chile peppers
1 avocado (optional)
1 clove garlic, finely minced
1 pound seafood of your choice, chopped
2 tablespoons olive oil
¼ cup freshly squeezed lime or lemon juice
2 tablespoons fresh cilantro, finely chopped
    (substitute 1 tablespoon dried cilantro)

Dice up the tomato (seeds discarded), scallions, green pepper (seeds removed), lime, and a green chile pepper or two. Add avocado, too, if you like, along with the minced garlic clove. Mix in a pound of chopped seafood of your choice—it should be as fresh as possible. Add olive oil, lime or lemon juice, and cilantro. This must be chilled and marinated until the seafood transforms from an uncooked, translucent appearance to a firm, "cooked" look, usually 4 to 6 hours. Drain most of the pickling liquid off and, to be fancy, serve in bowls resting in beds of ice.

Every region of Central America prides itself on its local version of Ceviche. In Costa Rica, they use an unusually tart orange (at least it looks like an orange) instead of limes, and they're heavy on the onions. In Baja Mexico, it's more like a tomato soup. In Panama, they add mayonnaise for a creamy, French look.

Pacific island Ceviche chefs do it "lomi lomi" style. For this, I prefer salmon, fresh as possible and sliced finely. If you're forced to use frozen salmon, use the most recent and let it thaw in the refrigerator and not at room temperature—there's no easier way to ruin frozen fish than to thaw it out quickly. It's similar to an unspicy ceviche, so you only marinate tomato, green onions, cucumber, and green pepper in lime juice. As before, let it pickle for about 4 hours. Oddly, this recipe was first served to me by a Bethel, Alaska, beach celebrity.

Buy a bag of limes for your boat next summer, with Ceviche and Lomi Lomi in mind. Both excel with freshly caught fish, and since the lime juice acts to pickle and preserve, it's easier to keep and use your catch.

Robon's 'Shroom Salad with Shrimp

This salad originated in Southeast Alaska, but it's from the sunny, hot sand and palm tree region. Chop fresh mushrooms, tomato, and cucumber. Add bean sprouts and sliced avocado. Snow peas are an option. Empty the contents of a jar of artichokes—the brand that contains olive oil and spices—into the mix. Then add Petersburg shrimp, or some similar delicacy. Add rice vinegar to taste. If you tire of shrimp, use poached and chilled halibut.

Pacifico Prawn and Avocado Soup

After being saladed out, it's time for mid-evening light meals. I found this first recipe in an Italian restaurant with a Polynesian name on the Pacific coast of Mexico. It's a clear, light soup and it's great. To serve 4, chop up 2 avocados and add 3 cups of fish stock. Throw in a prawn for each guest. Bring to a brief boil. Add a couple of jiggers of dry, white wine and the juice of a lemon. Serve it.

Salmon Lau Lau

Here's a modification of a light Polynesian meal. Take some salmon bellystrips and wrap them in taro leaves. Use spinach leaves if you're on the Mainland. You may want to use other types of fish and greens, such as mustard, chard, or wild greens— feel free. You may want to add a strip of bacon in the middle. Anyway, wrap the works in aluminum foil (or palm leaves if they're handy), and steam or bake for 15 minutes.

So if you're headed south this year, start now and get your stomach acclimated to the pleasures of saucy, tropical seafood fare. If you're not headed south, tack travel posters to the inside of your windows, set up the sunlamps, and these same vitamin-laden recipes will help you fight off cabin fever as well as the flus and colds of the frozen North. Either way, seafood makes it mo' betta.

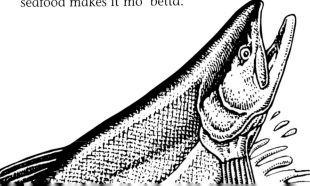

For us seafood lovers
whose manias tend
toward pyro...

CHAPTER 13
FLAMBÉING: SEAFOOD WITH A FLARE

For us seafood lovers whose manias tend toward pyro- and dipso-, flambéing brandies and other spirits lends an entertaining finishing touch to various fish entrees. Imagine, for example, blue brandy flames flickering over fillets of sole. Here, I will explain how to set your fish on fire and tell what fish tastes best with which liquors and spices.

How to Flambé

The secret of successful flaming dishes lies in heating the liquors before torching them. Other secrets include heating the serving platter and warming the dinner plate.

Two flambé methods are generally accepted. The first involves a long-handled pan with a cover. For each serving, use at least a jigger of booze. Heat the spirits in the covered pan until almost boiling. Remove the cover. Carefully touch a match to the side of the tilted pan and pour the flaming spirits over the serving dish or over the individual plates.

The second method employs a long-handled ladle. This technique works best if you have a gas cooking flame or fondue-type alcohol burner at or near the serving table.

Place the bowl of the empty ladle in the gas or alcohol flame and allow it to heat up. Then move the ladle well away from the fire and carefully pour some liquor into it. Wave the ladle of sizzling liquor back over the gas or fondue burner to ignite it. Now carefully ladle the flaming liquor over the cooked fish. You may have to repeat this several times if you're serving more than one or two people.

Cooking the Fish

Again, two methods are recommended. My favorite is to grill the fish on a barbecue. The grilled flavor complements the flaming liquor. Give some thought to using the liquor as a marinade before grilling, or consider adding a small amount of liquor while the fish is on the grill.

An alternative to grilling is to sauté the fish in a heavy skillet, using a small amount of butter or oil. It's easy to flambé the fish

in the skillet during the last stages of cooking. If you use this technique, you may want to make a sauce from the residual juices in the skillet. This works especially well with brandy and cognac.

Remove the fish from the skillet and keep it warm until serving time. Add about half as much flour as there is volume of butter-brandy remaining in the skillet. Let this bubble on medium heat for a minute or three. Then slowly add small portions of cream or soup stock, stirring all the while, until you like the looks of the sauce. This sauce is even better with parsley sprigs or sautéed mushrooms as garnish.

What Fish with What Spirits?

Many flaming fish recipes are of ethnic origin; tequila is used in Mexico, brandy in France, and so forth. Likewise, there are ethnic spices and regional fish species. I've compiled and tested a series of ethnic combinations, which are listed below:

- **Scandinavian:** The anise-based Pernod and anisette lend a licorice flavor that goes surprisingly well with salmon; fresh sprigs of dill serve as the spice and/or garnish.

- **French:** Brandy or cognac complements delicate fish such as sole, flounder, etc., and high-quality pink salmon fillets are a good substitute for sole. The almond flavor of amaretto makes a tasty flambé, but dilute one part amaretto with five parts brandy and the almond flavor will not overpower the others.

- **Mexican:** Use tequila and triple sec for the flames, red snapper for the fish, and cilantro for the spice; lime juice will add tartness and reinforce the triple sec.

- **Russian:** Vodka serves for both the marinade and the fire, on sturgeon or sablefish. Use garlic in the marinade and caviar and sliced, hard-boiled egg as garnish.

- **Caribbean:** Rum and orange juice make a nice marinade for grilled swordfish steaks, with curaçao for the flambé. Grated orange peel provides spice, and slices of orange can be used for garnish.

Now that you have a sense of the combinations of spirits, fish, and spices, let's run through some typical recipes. Here's my favorite, from a restaurant in Copenhagen:

Licorice Salmon

The hint of licorice and the sweetness of the liquor work magic on salmon. Grill salmon steaks on a charcoal barbecue. In a small, long-handled, covered saucepan, heat some anisette (at least 1 jigger per steak), along with some dill weed. Serve the steaks on a warm dish. Carefully ignite the anisette and pour it, flaming, over the steaks. Garnish with the chopped white portion of green onion and grated lemon peel. If you're really into this taste, serve with steamed fennel.

Lobster from the Sea of Cortez

Here's another sample recipe, this one from a Mexican restaurant on the Sea of Cortez. It calls for lobster, but try monkfish for a good substitute. The dish is prepared at tableside with a portable gas burner, some culinary showmanship, and a mariachi band for accompaniment.

First, remove the shell from the uncooked lobster. In a heavy skillet, sauté the lobster in a small amount of butter with a little freshly chopped garlic. Add a small shot of white wine and squeeze the juice from half an orange onto the lobster. Also add a small squirt from a bottle of triple sec and garnish with wedges of lime to give it a margarita flavor.

Serve the lobster on a warm plate and pour the skillet juices onto the meat. Then flambé the dish with tequila, using the hot ladle method. Serve with white wine.

In these flaming recipes, the spirits contribute more than just the entertainment value of blue flames flickering at mealtime. The flavor of these spirits mingles with the appropriate fish and complements the spices and garnishes.

RUN FOR THE HALIBUT

...I eat so much
that I don't know
what shoes
I'm wearing.

CHAPTER 14

LOW FAT AND HIGH FIBER: ANTIDOTES FOR GLUTTONY

1f I were to die tomorrow, Dante would have my first-class, smoking-section aisle seat in that special Ring of Hell designed to punish the Deadly Sin of Gluttony. Between seasonal feasts of Thanksgiving, Christmas, and New Year, I eat so much that I don't know what shoes I'm wearing. Then comes the Season of Penance and with it, I have a few eating resolutions and a few recipes of repentance.

Usually, my New Year's eating resolutions evolve from some basic tenets of healthy eating habits: low fat, seafood, high fiber. The high fiber in these recipes comes from beans, which contribute protein as well as flushing out your lower digestive tract. Bean eaters claim benefits in reducing weight, heart disease, colon problems, stress, and constipation—most all of our national diseases.

Low fat means using unsaturated, healthy olive oils and exorcising saturated animal fats or heavier plant oils. Olive oil contains no cholesterol and is said to clean fat deposits out of your arteries. I use two kinds of olive oils. First, use a light, cheap olive oil for high-temperature cooking, such as sautéing. Second, for salads and soups, I use a dark green, expensive oil, rich in fruity olive flavors otherwise destroyed by high temperatures.

When you're wrestling a heap of steaming crab, it's hard to toss butter from your diet. In those cases, I mix equal amounts of a light olive oil with melted butter. Another option for crab is ginger and soy dipping sauce, my favorite, even over butter. Simply shred a hunk of ginger and add soy sauce.

THE KRILL IS GONE

Clam and Bean Salad

In Alaska, late winter low tides beckon the foolhardy clam digger, armed with lantern and thermos, to brave snow and darkness for the savory bivalve. I'm not so foolhardy with my thermos—coffee hot as Hell and black as the Moor, with the faint aromas of brandy.

My favorite part of clam cookery is the cooking liquor or broth. I always make extra clam liquor and freeze it. It makes supreme cooking stock or you can quaff it straight up as hot soup. The clams in this recipe make low fat and high fiber less of a penance and more of a pleasure. This will serve up to 8 people.

First, dump a gallon bucket of clams into a large kettle and add about a half bottle of dry white wine. Cut the stems off a large bunch of cilantro and add those to the kettle. From a big handful of green onions, cut an inch off both the green ends and the white root ends. Add both of those to the kettle. Cover the kettle and boil the clams until they've opened up. Remove the clams and shell them.

Slowly decant the clam liquor from the kettle, taking care to leave the greens, sand, and sediment behind. Save ½ cup of the clam liquor for the dressing. I usually drink a ritual cup of clam broth before freezing the rest for later use.

This recipe calls for 4 cups of cooked white beans, also sold as cannellini beans, popular in Italy. If you use uncooked dry beans, use 2 cups or 1 pound. For cooking dried beans, remember the following bean-cooking hints:

- Soak beans 4 hours, changing the water at least once;
- Do not cook beans in the water you soaked them in;
- Do not add salt during soaking;
- White beans should be cooked from 60 to 90 minutes;
- Simmer beans, do not boil them;
- Olive oil will prevent frothing;
- Add water to keep beans covered during cooking; and
- Beans are done when you can mash one with your tongue.

If you use canned beans, rinse the beans well and discard the canned liquids.

For the salad, chop the green onions and cilantro left from making the clam liquor. Take a pound of snow peas and cut them each diagonally into thirds. Cut a red and green bell pepper into long slices.

For the dressing, use a blender or food processor to mix the half-cup of clam broth with 2 ounces of rice vinegar and a jigger of Rolls-Royce style mustard. With the blender on, slowly add 12 ounces of olive oil, the greenest in color you can find.

Mix the clams, beans, snow peas, greens, and peppers and toss with the dressing.

Egyptian Salmon and Fava Beans

It's the beans that are Egyptian. Those who built the pyramids flavored their fava beans with garlic and onion, as we're doing now. Before the other beans were introduced from the New World, fava beans had worked their way north into Switzerland and England during the Bronze and Iron Ages. We don't see many fresh fava beans in Alaska, but the canned variety can be found on some local supermarket shelves. Fava, also known as broad or horse beans, look like large lima beans.

In a large cast-iron skillet, quickly sauté 6 crushed garlic cloves in 2 ounces of green olive oil. Slice a red onion into thin rings and add them to the skillet. Before the onions have turned transparent, add 2 large cans of fava beans and ½ pound of chopped-up smoked salmon. Add a cup of fish stock or water, bring to a boil, and serve right away. Upon serving, add the juice of a lemon and garnish with thin slices of lemon. Serve with a dish of Bean Rouille alongside (recipe follows).

Bean Rouille

Rouille spices many fish dishes in the Mediterranean. Mostly rouille recipes call for mashed potatoes or wine-soaked bread as a base, but this version uses pureed beans. Rouille recipes also require cayenne pepper, lots of it.

You'll need a blender or food processor. Puree 1 cup of cooked cannellini (white) beans, ½ cup of roasted red bell peppers, 8 cloves of garlic, a big handful of dry cayenne peppers, and 2 ounces of olive oil. Rouille should flow like thick cream and inflame the taste buds with the fire of the cayenne inferno.

Rouille should be mixed into fish soups during cooking or be spread voluptuously onto croutons, which then float in soups.

Smoke-Alarm Beef Spinach Salad

Lean beef plays a role in my culinary recovery plan. Flank steak has very little fat to begin with and any that's left should be trimmed off. Feel free to substitute venison or other cuts of beef.

Slice 1 pound of meat into thin strips. Using a red-hot cast-iron skillet on the highest heat setting, braze the meat strips. Smoke plumes will rise and set off the fire alarms. You might warn the neighbors not to call the Fire Department. Remove the meat from the skillet and remove the skillet from the heat. Quickly add 2 ounces of raspberry vinegar to the hot skillet and scrape the skillet clean of attached steak residue. Add 4 ounces of green olive oil to the skillet.

In a large serving bowl, toss 1 pound of chopped fresh spinach leaves with a thinly sliced red onion, ½ pound of bean sprouts, a handful of capers, and 2 ounces of green olive oil. Then toss in the vinegar and oil mixture from the hot skillet and mix with the meat strips. Garnish with sliced hard-boiled eggs and freshly grated Parmesan cheese.

Fish and Fiber: Be Kind to Your Digestive Tract

The destiny of the human race rests in its colons and the stuff we put in them. That's what the fiber-philics would have us believe, and there's something to ponder. The cancer rate of the lower digestive tract in the United States is world record class. In the high-fiber-intake countries, the rate runs about 10 times lower. The evidence must be strong if a cereal manufacturer has enough confidence to advertise that their breakfast product fights cancer. These are not new ideas—the early Greeks regarded cabbage as the cleanser of the soul, if not merely the digestive tract.

Fiber is that stuff which we do not digest. It used to be known as roughage. Fiber originates from plants, seeds, nuts, grains, and vegetables. Examples include bran, barley, rice, corn, wheat, cabbage, celery, peppers, beans, onions, leeks, potatoes, broccoli, and the like. Things that do not contain fiber include meat, poultry, dairy products, and seafood. The health principle behind the fiber movement hinges upon a certain daily intake of fiber to prevent a buildup of havoc-wreaking substances loitering about in and inflicting damage to our intestines.

The health benefits of fiber manifest themselves in many ways, some of which cannot be glorified in polite company. Fiber itself is not very polite, impacting the senses but not the digestive tract. In addition to the lowered cancer rate claims, fiber eaters tend to show less fat, including cholesterol, in the bloodstream. High fiber users also tend to lose body weight.

The high fiber diet leads to other benefits besides health. Even with the most expensive "organic" grains and vegetables, the monthly food bills will likely drop. So will the monthly drugstore bills for laxatives and Preparation H.

These recipes combine the energy and healthful attributes of fiber with the taste and protein of seafood. Since some of the fiber foods seem to be a bit on the bland side, the recipes use extra-heavy doses of spices as antidotes.

Tabbouleh

This Mideastern salad, based upon cracked grains of wheat, has zip and spice when done right. To 2 cups of dried cracked or bulgur wheat, add 2 cups of boiling water, stir well, and let sit in the refrigerator in a large bowl for an hour. Meanwhile, chop up 1 bunch of green onions, 2 tomatoes, 1 small red onion, a bunch of parsley (or cilantro, especially if you add the optional seafood), 1 or 2 cloves of garlic, and a jalapeño pepper. Add the juice of 2 limes, ½ cup of olive oil, and a batch of either dried or freshly chopped mint. Once the bulgur wheat is chilled, mix up all these ingredients in the bowl. This is tabbouleh. So far, so good. Now for the seafood option. Mix in a pound of either Petersburg shrimp or chilled poached scallops. Much better.

Sweet-and-Sour Fish-and-Fiber

For an Asian or Russian flavor, this recipe yields a quick meal that gets better in the refrigerator after a while. In a large skillet, sauté 3 sliced onions in olive oil for 2 minutes, then add 1 small, shredded cabbage, 3 thinly sliced carrots, and 3 chopped tomatoes. After several more minutes, add ½ cup of rice vinegar, 2 ounces of honey, and ½ cup of fish stock. Arrange about a pound of chunked halibut on top of the vegetables, cover, and let steam for 10 to 15 minutes. This is best served chilled, with black bread or on brown rice.

Mariscos Enchiladas

Another Mexican-style dish, but nowhere as spicy. This one calls for squid, but should you want to pay more and get the same results, substitute lobster, scallops, or large prawns. In a large frying pan, sauté 1 large chopped onion and 1 garlic clove in olive oil. Once the onions are transparent, add 2 chopped tomatoes, a handful of chopped cilantro (substitute parsley), and a small chopped pepper. After a minute, add 1 pound of chopped cleaned squid and, stirring constantly, sauté just long enough to firm up the texture of the squid, probably less than 40 seconds. Serve on brown rice or bulgur.

Fajitas

This last Mexican-type meal fits in well for buffets serving large crowds. Slice white onions and bell peppers into long strips and sauté them in olive oil until they're soft. Place in a large serving dish and keep them warm. Then either broil or sauté, using the same oil, prawns (with shells removed), or chicken breasts, sliced into long strips, or beef, also sliced into long strips, or any combination of these. Again, place in a serving bowl and keep warm.

Make two sauces: a salsa and a guacamole. The salsa should be freshly made, although this keeps quite well for weeks in the refrigerator. I use this salsa on everything: eggs, sandwiches, fish, etc. Simply chop up green onions, red pepper, jalapeño pepper, chile pepper, yellow pepper, long pepper, short pepper, and any other pepper that's in the produce section. Add chopped tomatoes, chopped fresh cilantro (if you can't find fresh cilantro, also known as coriander or Chinese parsley, either grow some or apologize to your guests that this salsa is not complete), lime juice, and olive oil.

Make the guacamole by mashing very ripe avocados and mixing in lime juice and minced onion, and garlic. Again, set both sauces in serving bowls, keeping well chilled. Now warm up some flour tortillas, place all serving bowls on a table buffet-style, and announce the following rules:

1. Find a tortilla;
2. Place a small amount of onions and peppers on No. 1;
3. Place a small amount of prawn, chicken, beef, or combinations on No. 2;
4. Add salsa, guacamole, or both to No. 3;

5. Try to roll the No. 4 into a bite-size mass;

6. Eat No. 5, trying to contain the fallout for reuse.

Of course, the amounts and types of ingredients depend upon the population being fed and their ability to eat spicy or hot peppers and the like.

Quiche

Quiche provides the dish to mix and match a variety of high fiber vegetables with tasty seafoods and cheeses. This recipe fills two 9-inch pie plates. The basic beginnings use about 8 eggs and 1 pint of cream (or half-and-half), slightly beaten. Add nutmeg and white pepper if desired. Line the pie plates with pastry or use frozen store-bought pie shells. Here are the suggestions for vegetables, seafood, and cheeses; choose one or more from each group:

Vegetables: onions, zucchini, spinach, snow peas, broccoli, cauliflower, asparagus tips, peas

Seafood: scallops, salmon (smoked or poached), crab

Cheeses: mozzarella, provolone, Romano, Swiss (grated)

Once you've filled the pie plates with assorted vegetables and seafood and topped that with grated cheese, flood the plate with the egg-cream mixture and bake in a preheated oven at 400°F for 20 to 30 minutes. The quiche is done when an inserted knife blade comes out clean. Try quiches for Sunday brunches with lots of champagne.

The Last Word

The healthy atonements of low-fat, high-bean recipes may postpone my date with Dante for a while, when I may be able to choose another seat in another Ring. Meanwhile, to keep in practice, I'll maintain an ample intake of Rouille. And if anyone gives you any macho crap about real men not eating quiche, remember that they're probably constipated and you're not.

SECTION 3
EATING ALASKA: INDIGENOUS FOODS

To get the best taste for Coastal Alaska, you should eat it. Get to know the flavor of Coastal Alaska through the senses of smell and taste as well as through the senses of sight and sound. The salmon, seaweed, halibut, crab, the mussels and clams, and the plants that grow on the beach—these are the things you'll remember and long for.

At last,
a nutrition craze
that promotes
canned salmon.

CHAPTER 15

SALMON: AN OLD-STYLE ALASKA STAPLE REVISITED

In the old days, most Alaskans canned their fish products. Nowadays, we can deliver fresh or flash-frozen, even though the faithful are still "putting up" caseloads of fish to last the winter. There are some benefits for using the canned versions—think of it as canned calcium—and if you can take a hint, these recipes will work for you.

At last, a nutrition craze that promotes canned salmon. And at the height of the craze, guess who has several million cases of canned salmon handy? Now to convince several million fish-eaters that human bones won't crumble in old age if only they would eat salmon bones now.

Osteoporosis, a serious bone disease facing aging women, can be prevented by increasing calcium intake in midlife. "Brittle bone" disease remains epidemic among American women, the leading cause of death for those over 65.

Canned salmon provides a great calcium source—on an equal weight basis, more than milk. But canned salmon must contain the bones; otherwise the calcium content is almost nil.

First, some general notes on calcium in life and everyday cooking:

- Avoid foods high in phosphorus, such as red meat and fowl, which hinder calcium uptake;
- Smoking and alcohol also hinder calcium uptake, so more calcium will be needed for the addicted;
- Use powdered skim milk, instead of "nondairy creamers," for coffee;
- Crumble dried seaweed leaves and sprinkle them over dishes as a calcium-rich salt substitute;

- Add grated Parmesan cheese to dishes whenever you can;
- Add a dash of powdered skim milk to dishes whenever possible;
- Some foods inhibit calcium uptake: avoid kale, mustard greens, chocolate, and bran;
- Use yogurt instead of sour cream;
- Use ricotta instead of cream cheese.

Now for the recipes. With calcium in mind, I've put together some innovative canned salmon recipes with a lot of high-calcium ingredients. Remember: don't throw out the bones—the canning process makes them edible.

Salmon Kelp Salad

Rehydrate store-bought kelp, often sold as "wakame," by steeping in hot water, or harvest some wing kelp (alaria—attached to rocks at mid-tide, recognized by the stemlike rib in the middle of the leaflike fronds) off the beach. Chop the kelp into small pieces. Blend into a can of salmon, flaked. Add this blend to a bed of lettuce. Make a dressing by adding an ounce of miso to a cup of mayonnaise. Spread this over the kelp-salmon mixture. Garnish with chunks of tofu, lemon slices, and parsley.

Salmon Asparagus Soup

Cut fresh asparagus spears into inch-long chunks and sauté in ¼ cup of olive oil until just tender, but still crunchy. Add a ¼ cup of flour and mix until a paste is formed. Then add 1 or 2 cups of water to thin it out a bit. Add a 1-pound can of salmon to the mixture, including the can juices. Once warmed up to bubbling, thin with a cup or so of cream or milk, reheat for a minute, and serve. For extra flavor, add dried asparagus soup mix instead of flour. If you like broccoli, more better. Follow the above steps, using broccoli. It's just as good and you get more calcium. Some health folks claim broccoli prevents cancer, too.

Spinach Salmon Salad

Drain and flake a 1-pound can of salmon, including bones. Add 1 pound of washed and torn fresh spinach leaves. Chop up a couple heads of broccoli and two handfuls of mushrooms. Toss with a dill-and-yogurt dressing: 1 cup of yogurt with 1 ounce of mayonnaise, a handful of chopped green onions, 1 tablespoon of mustard, and 1 tablespoon of chopped fresh dill (or 1 teaspoon of dried dill). Mix well.

Salmon Nicoise

In a large mixing bowl, add 1 cup of drained chopped olives—using several varieties of olives—to 2 chopped and deseeded tomatoes, 1 large chopped red onion, a sliced red bell pepper, a sliced green bell pepper, and a handful of chopped parsley. Mix this well with a vinaigrette (equal amounts of olive oil and lemon juice, a couple finely minced garlic cloves, chopped capers, and a dash of Dijon mustard). Tear a head of red leaf or romaine lettuce into bite-sized pieces and arrange them in a bowl. Then place the vegetable mixture in a mound on the lettuce. Now drain and flake a 1-pound can of salmon and place the salmon on top of the vegetable mound. Then garnish with chunks of feta cheese, chopped olives, capers, and maybe an anchovy fillet—or maybe not an anchovy. Dump more vinaigrette onto it and serve under hot sunlamps.

Salmon-Stuffed Potatoes

Chop up an onion and green bell pepper and sauté them in olive oil until the onions are transparent. Take a couple of baked potatoes and carefully scoop out the insides. In a mixing bowl, mash the insides and mix in a can of salmon. Stir in yogurt, grated cheddar cheese, and the sautéed vegetables. Restuff the baked potatoes with this mixture and return to the oven for 15 minutes. Garnish with chopped green onion or parsley.

Other Canned Salmon Ideas

Try canned salmon with spaghetti or other pastas. Mix it into scrambled eggs, quiches, and frittatas. Think of canned salmon as a substitute for ham, using it in bean soups, already high in calcium. Just remember, this isn't like canned salmon of olde. This is the reborn, high-calcium canned salmon, hero of the latest nutrition movement. There's a big difference—you can feel it in your bones.

Uncanned: A Salmon Tour of Europe

From the dill of the North to the garlic of the South and the curry of the East, our cosmopolitan friend salmon receives a different welcome in each part of Europe. Of course, all Europeans treat the salmon with respect and a gourmet touch. Here are some recipes from several European countries to give you an idea of the variety of receptions that a salmon might see on its European tour.

England

The brisk morning of a foxhunt: what's the traditional breakfast? Try using smoked salmon in curry-flavored Kedgeree. Begin by boiling up a mix of white and wild rice and cooking some hard-boiled eggs. Now heat up some flaked smoked salmon (actually, canned salmon will do as a substitute) in plenty of extra fish stock (made with white wine, water, thyme, pepper, garlic cloves, diced onions, and carrots—if in a hurry, just use the wine and water; if in a rush, omit the water).

Meanwhile, make a Curry Sauce: for each cup of sauce, melt 1 tablespoon of butter, and blend in 1 tablespoon of flour and 1 teaspoon of curry powder; stir this for 2 minutes, then slowly add 1 cup of the extra fish stock and 2 jiggers of pale, dry sherry, still stirring. Separate the cooked eggs into yolks and whites and grate each. Mix up the cooked rice and warmed smoked salmon in a large warm dish; pour the curry sauce on top. Decorate by garnishing with chopped chives (or green onions) and the grated egg yolks and whites. Serve with chutney. *Tally-ho.*

France

What else? In Paris, you'd poach salmon in champagne, with caviar. This recipe calls for a salmon roe caviar. The poaching liquid uses about half a bottle of dry champagne and the same amount of water, thyme, bay leaves, crushed black pepper, a dash of white wine vinegar, well-washed chopped green parts of leeks, a chopped carrot, and some thinly sliced celery, including the leafy parts. Boil the stock for 20 minutes.

Place a salmon fillet in a cooking dish and add enough poaching liquid to cover the fish. Use more champagne if necessary. If not, drink it.

Cover the dish and continue to simmer until the fish is done, 10 minutes per inch of fish thickness. When the fish flakes easily and is still slightly pink in the center, remove the fish from the heat but keep warm.

Remove some of the poaching liquid and vegetables and puree them in a blender or food processor. Simmer this in a frying pan until the volume is reduced by half. Add an equal volume of cream and simmer it further until it looks like sauce. Serve the fish with the sauce on top, garnishing with about ½ pound of salmon roe caviar. A watercress garnish accompanies the salmon roe nicely. More champagne is also necessary.

Another French treatment of salmon uses a sorrel-type garnish and basically the same sauce as above, substituting dry white wine for champagne, omitting carrots and celery, and using the white parts of leeks rather than the green parts.

Remove the skin from the salmon fillet and cut it into serving-sized chunks. Place the salmon chunks between 2 pieces of wax paper and, using a large spatula or the flat side of a cleaver, gently mash or pound the salmon chunk until it's about ½ inch thick. Sauté the flattened chunk in butter, about a half-minute for each side.

Serve with the sauce on top and garnish with finely chopped sorrel. (Around inhabited areas of Alaska, a sorrel relative can be found growing wild as sourdock; otherwise, substitute chopped spinach mixed with freshly squeezed lemon juice.)

Scandinavia

Moving north into dill country, salmon becomes more common. A sandwich serving uses smoked salmon. Start by mixing ½ cup of sour cream with a tablespoon of horseradish and freshly ground white pepper. Spread this mixture on thinly sliced rye bread. Cover with several thin slices of smoked salmon. Then add a layer of sliced radishes and a layer of thinly sliced cucumbers. Top off each sandwich with a sprig of dill.

An easy Scandinavian touch simply means adding a dill sauce to poached salmon. The simple dill sauce mixes chopped dill with sour cream. Another utility dill sauce uses 2 cups of peeled, deseeded cucumber chunks, 2 cups of fresh dill pieces, a mashed and chopped garlic clove, 1 cup of sour cream, 1 cup of mayonnaise, and cayenne pepper to taste, all blended in a food processor. Use sprigs of dill and cucumber and lemon slices for garnish.

Italy

In Italy, they pinch the salmon before serving it. Salmon Risotto is a rice dish, but it's definitely an Italian rice dish. Follow the rice cooking procedure exactly. Flake about ½ pound of smoked salmon and sauté it in ½ stick of butter for 2 minutes. Pour about half of the butter into another large saucepan for later use. To the salmon-butter mixture, add a jigger of brandy and simmer until the liquid is almost gone. Add ½ cup of cream, simmer for 1 minute, and set aside. *Read on . . .*

Now, in the other saucepan, sauté a chopped onion and a minced garlic clove in the butter until the onions are translucent. Then add 2 cups of white rice and sauté for 1 or 2 minutes so that each rice grain is opaque and coated with butter. Add more butter if necessary, but do not let it brown.

Now add about ½ cup of hot fish stock and cook over medium heat until the stock is almost gone. Tireless stirring is necessary. No rice may stick to the bottom. Add more fish stock as the previous batch dries out, but never let too much fish stock build up. The rice should be more steamed than boiled. Continue to add fish stock in ½ cup batches until about 6 cups are used. The temperature should be hot enough to use up 6 cups of stock in about 20 minutes. Be careful near the end of the cooking cycle so that you don't end up with any unabsorbed fish stock.

The rice should be creamy, tender but firm to the bite; it should not be dry (temperature too high) or gluey (too low). Now mix in the salmon-butter mixture previously set aside. Toss in a handful of grated Parmesan cheese and top with several sprigs of parsley.

Turkey

Pilaf originated in the East, and this is a Turkish recipe. Notice the differences between pilaf and risotto: for pilaf, the rice is not stirred and the liquid is added all at once. Soak 1 cup of rice for 2 hours in strongly salted water. In plenty of butter, sauté a medium chopped yellow onion until transparent.

Drain the rice well, add to the onions, and sauté for a few minutes but without browning the butter. Mix in 1 pound of flaked smoked salmon, and place everything in a casserole dish. Using a hot fish stock with a tablespoon of curry powder and some white wine added, fill the casserole dish so as to cover the rice-salmon mixture with 1 inch of stock. Bake at 350°F for 45 minutes. Add more fish stock if it evaporates too quickly. Serve with chopped almonds.

Another salmon curry recipe from the East, this one quickly done. Sauté a bunch of chopped green onions in butter for a few minutes. Add a teaspoon of grated ginger, 1 cup of flaked salmon, ½ cup of sake (or sherry), 2 cups of green pea soup (instant, canned, or from scratch), and 2 tablespoons of curry powder. Mix well; heat until all is cooked. Serve with rice and chutney.

CHAPTER 16

HERRING: MORE TO LIFE THAN BEING PICKLED

When you're hip deep in herring, it's hard to think of eating them. But herring have been the staple of many people's diets for centuries. In Alaska, the return of the herring marks the opening of spring, the return to the sea, the forerunner of the salmon that follow them. This year try herring as foodstuff. Guidance and advice follow.

The Pacific herring, twice the size of the Atlantic version, serves as prey for almost every voracious predator in and above the sea. A turmoil of activity betrays the schools of herring, as wide-eyed, hysterical beasts gorge themselves into orgasms of bloodthirsty gluttony. The intensity of such a biological tempest would astonish the innocent spectator.

Several years ago, the herring were so thick in Auke Bay in Southeast Alaska that the sea lions chased the herring under the docks. The killer whales followed and chased the sea lions onto the docks. The eagles swooped to snatch talons-full of herring, and the seagulls fought for the scraps. The children were jigging, catching several herring per cast, and the adults were cursing the sea lions for tangling the nets. Quite a show.

With that much predation, the herring would have to be as prolific as rabbits to survive. Herring begin to spawn in late March or early April in Southeast Alaksa, and later as you move northward. The eggs are deposited near the intertidal zone, with the best chances of success for those eggs being affixed to seaweed. It takes about four years for a herring to mature. A female herring will release from 10,000 to 60,000 eggs each year, averaging four years as an adult spawner.

MAN WITH

HERRING AID

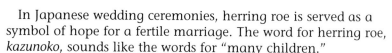

In Japanese wedding ceremonies, herring roe is served as a symbol of hope for a fertile marriage. The word for herring roe, *kazunoko*, sounds like the words for "many children."

Herring is a relatively high-fat, high-calorie fish. In the spring, the herring are lean and best used for smoking. Later in the fall, the fat content reaches a maximum and the herring are better used for pickling or cooking. Herring are also high in calcium content—twice as high as milk on an equal weight basis.

Freshly caught herring should be eaten within two days, but can be easily frozen whole for a year. Herring can be salted by alternating layers of fish and salt or in a saturated brine solution (mix no more than 4 pounds of salt per gallon of water). To use salted herring, soak them overnight in several rinses of fresh water.

Kippered herring (salted and smoked herring) can be desalted the same way. Some experts use half milk and half water for desalting. If salted herring are to be cooked, you can desalt them more quickly by pouring boiling water over them.

Herring can be easily smoked. After salting for 24 hours, run a rod through the gills and hang them in a smoker, using high heat and alder chips. After being sufficiently dried out, the herring can be split in two, deboned, and trimmed of guts and head. The Irish take several such smoked herring, place them in a pan, pour whiskey over them to cover, and ignite the whiskey. When the flames go out, it's ready to eat.

Pickled Herring

Most recipes start with salted herring, freshened (desalted with milk and water), beheaded, and deboned. To skin or not to skin is your first option. Chunks of herring are alternated with layers of red onion (and option No. 2, carrot slices) in a jar. Spices normally added include bay leaves, whole peppers, allspice, and sometimes whole cloves and lemon slices. Fill the jar with a solution of 3 parts white wine (or normal white vinegar) to 1 part white sugar (or brown) to 1 part water. This solution is sometimes boiled first and cooled. Allow to pickle from about a half-day to 2 days before using. If refrigerated, the pickled herring should last several months.

Pickled Herring are excellent when served mixed in with a Curried Mayonnaise: to 1 cup of mayonnaise, add 2 teaspoons of curry powder, ¼ teaspoon of ground coriander, and ¼ teaspoon of ground turmeric. Drain the pickling juices from the herring before mixing with the curried mayonnaise.

Herring Salad

No smorgasbord is complete without it. Boil potatoes and eggs in one pan. In another, boil fresh, peeled beets (some recipes call for canned pickled beets, but try it with fresh beets). Both potatoes and beets should not be soft, but stay on the crunchy side. Dice the potatoes and beets. Slice the eggs and set them aside. Chop an onion and a tart apple. Dice finely a dill pickle. Mix all the above with pickled herring, olive oil, and white wine vinegar. Garnish with the slices of egg and sprigs of parsley and serve on a bed of greens.

Leftover Herring Salad Soup

This is something to be tried for any salad. Peel and slice a potato and sauté it in butter. Add a pint of fish stock or bouillon. Now add 2 cups of leftover Herring Salad, as above, including the dressing. Add spices, such as basil, oregano, etc. Boil for 10 minutes. Place all this in a blender and homogenize it. You'll be pleasantly surprised, trust me.

Escabeche

Ingredients:

1 ounce olive oil
1 pound herring fillet, skinless and deboned, in 1-inch chunks
1 onion, chopped
1 small carrot, chopped
4 garlic cloves, whole
6 ounces wine vinegar
2 small hot red peppers
1 bay leaf
Dash thyme
2 ounces water

When in Spain, the herring is pickled like this. In hot olive oil, sauté the chunks for 5 seconds, leaving them no more than half done. Remove from the pan and in the same oil, sauté the onion, carrot, and garlic. When the onions turn transparent, add the wine vinegar, peppers, bay leaf, thyme, and water. After simmering for 5 minutes, pour the sauce over the herring chunks and refrigerate for 24 hours.

Fish Balls / Fish Pudding

Back to the Scandinavian countries, this versatile dish can use most any fish and turn out as pudding too. Take 1 pound of deboned, skinless fillet of herring and grind in a food processor, blender, or grinder until a paste forms. Add 1 ounce of potato flour, 1 ounce of regular flour, and 3 tablespoons of butter. Spice with freshly ground white pepper and a pinch of nutmeg or ginger, if desired. Blend for 10 seconds. Slowly add 1 pint of cream while blending. This mixture can be formed into balls and fried or boiled.

To prepare as pudding, omit the butter and spoon the mixture into a shallow pan and cover tightly with foil. Set in a larger pan containing at least 1 inch of water. Place in an oven set at 350°F for 30 minutes. Serve with boiled and buttered potatoes or with a shrimp sauce: melt 1 ounce of butter and stir in 1 ounce of flour; before the flour turns brown, slowly add and stir in 1 cup of cream; add white pepper and dill; add 1 cup of shrimp.

Grape-Leaf Herring

Dampen your grape leaves. If you're temporarily out of grape leaves, use broad-leaf seaweed. Otherwise, use foil. Using whole herring, guts removed, marinate the fish in a mixture of 4 parts olive oil, 1 part Pernod (or anisette), and fennel leaves for at least 1 hour. Wrap each fish in the grape leaves and grill over hot coals, turning once, cooking several minutes on each side.

Mustard Grilled Herring, English-Style

Slit the fresh, degutted herrings along the back and sides. Coat them with mustard and sprinkle with bread crumbs. Cook them slowly under the broiler or over coals. Serve with Mustard Sauce: melt 1 ounce butter, add 1 ounce flour, and stir in 1 cup of water. Stir vigorously and add 1 egg yolk mixed with 1 tablespoon of cold water. Over low heat, add 4 ounces of butter, cut into small pieces, stirring all the time, then add ¼ cup of mustard.

Scottish-Style Fried Herring

Using fresh herring, either whole or split and deboned, cut off the head, tail, and fins. Then roll them in Scotch oatmeal. Fry in olive oil. Serve with lemon wedges or Mustard Sauce, above.

Herring Roe

A great delicacy in Japan, sac roe causes fishermen and their spotter aircraft pilots to go into a harvesting frenzy on their own. Some prefer it cooked. Parboil roe by simmering in white wine for 5 minutes. Carefully remove any membranes. It can now be sautéed in butter or poached, served on toast. Roe goes well mixed in with scrambled eggs. Roe can be salted in brine (4 pounds of salt per gallon) for later use. To freshen, rinse with several changes of fresh water and milk as directed at the beginning of this chapter.

Roe on Kelp

Should you be able to snag some herring egg-laden kelp, hang on to it. Dip it into boiling water for a second. Then eat it. Soy sauce or melted butter adds to it. This would cost you $10 a leaf in a Tokyo restaurant.

THE LORD KELPS THOSE

THAT KELP THEMSELVES

As has been shown, the diversity of herring-as-food extends into many cultures. There is life beyond pickled herring. The seas have no substitute for the herring; it is the pivotal link of the food chain. Ten thousand predators can't be wrong. Try herring yourself, in one form and another.

Chapter 17
Oysters: Food for Lovers

Oysters have fueled the passions of lovers throughout time. Wall paintings of early Greeks and Romans depict oysters playing their part in the famous banquets and orgies of those days. Casanova, the prolific Italian lover of the 1700s, attributed his prowess to oysters—he ate 50 for breakfast each day.

Oysters provide nutrients for more than just the pursuits of Eros. The aphrodisiac qualities of oysters are ascribed to their phosphorus, calcium, iodine, iron, and vitamin B contents. All of these have side effects to benefit our basic health. Oysters also contain vitamins A and C and are prescribed as cures for anemia and goiter, and as the means to clear skin and to lengthen life. Oysters also have been known as brain food. Cicero ate oysters before oration, and the enlightened Louis XI required his crew of French intellectuals to eat a daily diet of this brain food.

Alaskan oysters merit special attention. Our waters are too cold for oysters to reproduce naturally, so oyster spat must be introduced to seed oyster farms. However, our cold water benefits us in two ways. First, all of the oyster's energy is directed toward building tasty body tissue rather than toward reproductive tissue. Second, there's no reason to suspend harvesting during the summer reproductive season. I find Alaskan oysters to be firm, crunchy, and deliciously salty.

Normally, oysters are eaten raw, fried, baked, or stewed. I'll avoid most of the normal oyster recipes because they're too normal and uninspiring. If you're looking for inspired oyster recipe reading, try M. F. K. Fisher's *Consider the Oyster* for her witty anecdotes, delightful prose, and obvious adoration of the oyster.

LOVE AT FIRST BITE

To Stew Right the Oyster

The problem with stews is that the oysters can be too easily overcooked. This simple recipe avoids that. Feel free to embellish this stew with potatoes, celery, onions, and other ingredients, but cook them separately before adding them to the oyster stew. Prepare your heaviest metal stew pot by bringing to a bare simmer a volume of milk, 1 cup to a customer. Then set a heavy iron skillet over medium-high heat. For each serving, add 1 tablespoon of butter and allow it to melt, bubble, and foam. Before the butter browns, add 4 drained oysters per serving to the skillet, and stir while frying for a minute. The edges will curl and the oysters will plump up before your eyes. Delicious oyster liquor will appear and join in the froth.

After a minute, dump the butter, liquor, and oysters into the stew pot of simmering milk and immediately remove the stew pot from the heat. Serve these corpulent morsels quickly, with a glass of sherry on the side and maybe a splash of sherry in the stew.

Oysters Roasting on an Open Fire

Between two beach logs, build a blazing fire and let it burn down to hot coals. Add foil-wrapped corn and potatoes to the coals and place a grill over the beach logs. Place the oysters, still in their shells, atop the grill. Place a steel cup on the grill and melt some butter in it. When the heat causes the shells to open, remove them from the grill. Bring along gloves (for handling hot oyster shells), a knife (to cut oyster muscles), forks, lemons, hot sauce, and cold beer. If you can't get to the beach, use your barbecue pit.

Stir-Frying the Gingered Oysters

Prepare a marinade/thickening sauce by grating a thumb-sized hunk of ginger and squeezing the juice into a bowl. To the bowl, add 1 ounce of soy sauce, 3 ounces of sake (or dry sherry), and 1 tablespoon of cornstarch. Stir until the cornstarch dissolves. Add a dozen oysters and marinate for 30 minutes.

Meanwhile, chop a bunch of green onions into inch-long sections. Peel another thumb-sized hunk of ginger and chop it into matchstick-sized strips. Using a wok or heavy iron skillet, quickly sauté the onion and ginger in 1 ounce of olive oil. Remove them, leaving most of the oil. Now drain the oysters and sauté them for 2 minutes, until the oysters have plumped up. Remove the oysters, leaving their liquor in the wok.

Slowly add the remaining marinade/thickening sauce and stir until the sauce has thickened. Once the sauce has thickened and is simmering, return the onions, ginger, and oysters to the wok. Reheat and serve over rice.

Pickling the Oyster, the Nippon Way

For each dozen oysters, boil them for a minute in the juice of half a lemon and a splash of water. Drain off the liquids. Now sauté the oysters in 2 ounces of olive oil. When the oysters have plumped up and their edges have curled, remove them from the oil. Add 2 chopped garlic cloves and 6 crushed peppercorns to the oil and sauté this until the garlic has just softened. Mix up the oysters, garlic, and peppercorns in a bowl with 1 ounce of rice vinegar, a jigger of sake, 1 teaspoon of honey, and 12 drops of Tabasco sauce. Add the juice of half a lemon and marinate, chilled, for several hours. Serve with more sake.

Oysters with Roux

Sauté a dozen oysters over moderate to low heat in butter until they plump up, usually a minute or three. Add a cup of cream. Thicken with 1 ounce of roux (see Chapter 8 for a couple of roux versions), add a jigger of dry sherry, and a dash of Tabasco.

On the next Valentine's Day, let us celebrate our Basic Inalienable Rights: life, love, and the pursuit of oysters.

OYSTERS: FOOD FOR LOVERS

Chapter 18
The Edible Mussel

The magnificent blue mussel, with the Latin name *Mytilus edulis*—the edible mussel—now appears in gourmet seafood shops and fish markets near you. By far one of the top delicacies in France, the blue mussel has been, for some perplexing reason, neglected in the United States. The cosmopolitan edible mussel abounds at mid-tides on rocky shorelines around the world, is easily pried off, far more accessible and far less work than clams. And much more delectable.

There's a big difference between beach-pried mussels and store-bought "cultivated" mussels. Cultivated mussels are plump, soft, and pampered, the result of having spent their sheltered childhoods on plush floating mussel racks, constantly submerged and feeding, protected from waves and predators. Juneau supermarkets and Anchorage specialty stores also feature the New Zealand green-lipped mussel. This cultivated variety is outstanding. Beach mussels are leaner and tougher, exposed to waves, starfish, and borers, and high and dry half the time. But both the cultivated and beach mussels share a common denominator: they're delicious.

To prepare mussels, simply clean off the crud with a wire brush. Next, most people remove the "beard"—those threads that the mussels use to attach themselves to rocks. If you're just going to dip steamed mussels in butter, leave the beard to hold onto (and then discard). They're easier to remove after steaming anyhow.

Herbed Steamed Mussels with Wine Sauce

The easiest mussel recipes are often the best. Steam a potful in 1 inch of dry, white wine. Add tarragon and thyme. Shuck only those with open shells. Simply dip the mussels in butter or make a sauce: to 1 tablespoon of melted butter, add 1 tablespoon of flour; slowly add about a cup of the pot liquor and cream to suit the consistency and taste you prefer.

Make toast: I sauté sliced French bread in olive oil. Stack the mussels on the toast and load the sauce on top. Pour about 8 inches of the wine in a jam jar and go for it.

How about Pickled Mussels? A British Columbia treat: fill a jar with shucked steamed mussels and add malt vinegar. Spices are optional. Refrigerate for several days until they're ready. They keep for a long time if cooled.

Charcoal-Smoked Mussels

On a barbecue grill or on a grate above an alder beach fire, simply place a handful of mussels and wait for them to open. Throw some garlic cloves on the fire if you're that type of person. For a sauce, dip the mussels in melted butter and then dredge them in a bowl of Parmesan cheese and celery seeds. With the smoked variety, beer is preferred by most musselphiles.

And then there's . . .

Suzanne's Mussel Soup

Lightly sauté some shallots (substitute leeks or mild onions if you're out of shallots) in olive oil, adding crushed garlic and tarragon. Add some red wine and vinegar and simmer for a few minutes. Now add a can or two of Italian tomatoes and a few chopped jalapeño peppers. Toss in your supply of mussels, still in their shells. Add red wine to cover and simmer until the shells open up. Red wine goes well. Try a zinfandel.

Russel's Mussel Spinach Salad

If you're a salad freak, try this one. The secret lies in a questionable family vinaigrette recipe of uncertain origin. Shred 1 large peeled hunk of ginger root and 12 garlic cloves. Add tarragon. Add 1 cup of safflower oil, ½ ounce of sesame oil, and ½ cup of rice vinegar. Then add 25 twists of freshly ground pepper. Mix this well. Soak some steamed mussels in chilled vinaigrette for several hours and toss in some chopped fresh spinach.

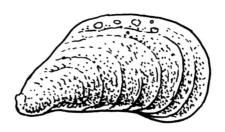

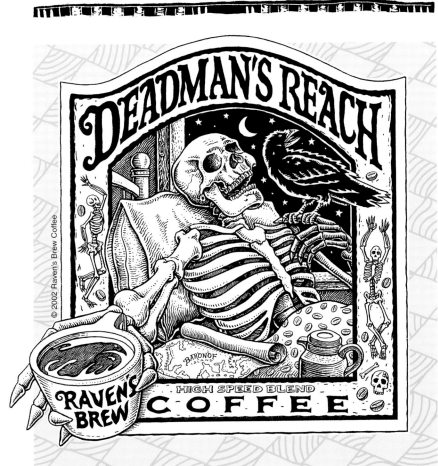

© 2002 Raven's Brew Coffee

Red Tide Caution

Mussels and PSP? You bet! Mussels are filter feeders that strain out those toxic red tide algae with the best of them. And the toxins linger on well after the red tide. In fact, it was mussels that did in 150 Aleuts in aptly named Poison Cove and Deadman's Reach on the south coast of Baranof Island in 1799. I'm real cautious about beach mussels, even in the winter before the spring algae blooms. Mussels are not in good shape then anyhow.

All the more reason to go for the store-bought cultivated mussels. But if you must pick beach mussels, be close to a hospital, know CPR, and let someone else test out a small portion of a mussel before wholesale consumption. It only takes a half hour or so to detect the symptoms: tingling or numbness in lips, inability to breathe, etc.

Cajun Mussels Paella

For mussel lovers of Creole extraction, try this paella recipe.

Ingredients for 4 servings:

¼ cup white wine
⅛ teaspoon saffron threads (about $60 worth)
1 white onion, chopped
4 cloves garlic, minced
¼ teaspoon ground red pepper
1 ounce butter
1 cup long-grained white rice
1 pound tomatoes, peeled and chopped
½ cup chicken stock
Thyme to taste
Hot pepper sauce to taste
1 pound okra
1 pound green and red bell peppers, thinly sliced
1 pound mussels
½ pound shrimp
½ pound halibut, in chunks
Chopped parsley to taste
Lemon juice to taste

A
MUSSEL
MAN

Heat up the white wine and add the saffron; let that stand for 20 minutes. Meanwhile, sauté the onion and garlic with the dry red pepper in the butter. After about a minute, add the long-grain rice. After another minute, add the tomatoes, chicken stock, thyme, and hot pepper sauce, and the wine/ saffron mixture. Boil, then simmer for about 18 minutes. Add the okra and bell peppers. Now add the mussels, shrimp, and halibut. Cover and cook until the seafood is done. Toss the mixture and top it off with chopped parsley and juice of a lemon. Serve it right now.

After you've tried mussels, you'll never be able to look the intertidal zone in the eye again without marveling at what treats have been provided in such abundance. Don't neglect the edible mussel.

CHAPTER 19

SHRIMP, SCALLOPS, SNAPPER: RECIPES RATED 'X'

Sex and violence. You see them on TV. You read about them in newspapers. They invade every seam of life. Why not use them in cooking? The sensuous nature of seafood makes for delicious titillations of taste. Those suggestions may sound a bit kinky, but don't be quick to criticize until you've experienced them.

You can't think about violence without thinking about abalone. But beating abs with a mallet is no longer camp. The neighbors will call the cops. Annabel, who knows about such things, has told me about the "in" ways to subdue the toughest ab without arousing suspicion. Lay out a clean piece of lumber, say a 2-by-8, in the driveway. Place your abs on the plank. Lay another 2-by-8 on top. Drive over the planks with your car. Still violent, but with more class. And talk about tender! Then proceed "normally" with an abalone recipe. My choice is to sauté them, unbreaded, for a very short time, say 50 seconds total, in hot butter.

Shrimp Tempura

Not violent enough for you? Try battered shrimp. Tempura batter should be tried for an Eastern twist. Use about equal parts of flour and ice-cold water. Slowly add the flour to the water, whipping vigorously but quickly. Leave the batter a bit lumpy. Tear the heads off the little shrimp bodies and rip their shells off, except for the last meatless section of tail. Split their backs down almost to their bellies with a sharp knife, and pull their veins out. Dredge them in the batter and immerse them in boiling oil: 450°F as measured by a thermometer. If too many pieces are added at once, the temperature falls and the batter cooks up limp.

Into "S and M"? How about a racy recipe for shrimp and mussels?

Pagan Paella

From the kitchen of the depraved Maestro comes a Pagan Paella, rich in red ribaldry. Start with a large, heavy, black iron skillet with a matching cover. In lots of olive oil, lightly sauté 1 large onion, 1 well-endowed zucchini, 1 big red bell pepper, and 2 cloves of garlic, all chopped. Add 2 peeled and chopped tomatoes, 1 cup of cooked white rice, and 1 cup of shelled peas. Arrange a dozen unshelled, beheaded shrimp and 2 dozen de-bearded, unshelled mussels around the skillet. Cover with water (and red wine unless you're strange). Add all the saffron you can afford, 2 ounces of paprika, and as much cayenne pepper as your masochistic tastes can tolerate. Cover and steam until the mussels give up and expose themselves.

I know too much violence can be disgusting, so let's move into the more sensuous aspects of seafood. This next trick can be used in almost any situation. It reminds me of the old Mazola-and-Visqueen parties of our college days, yet you can do it in your kitchen so long as you don't enjoy yourself too much. In one hand, take whatever fish you intend to cook. With your other, reach deeply into a mayonnaise jar and take a whole handful of mayonnaise (for real nostalgia, use mayonnaise made from corn oil) and, with closed eyes, gently caress and rub the fish all over with the mayo. Massage in a cup of chopped cilantro. Take your time and relish the moment. Then cook as "normal" in most any recipe. I like it baked or grilled, but poaching doesn't work. (This recipe was sensuously related to me on my yacht by Bonnie Raitt. She's cleaned up her act since then.)

No discussion of sex and seafood can be complete without talking about milt and roe. Both are gourmet items and should be cherished. Salmon caviar is just as good as any other, and salmon milt, which is much sought after in Europe, is surprisingly good—reminding one of Rocky Mountain oysters, but much better. Here are some exotic treatments.

First, about milt, North American Natives ate it raw, claiming increased virility. Milt is much better named as "soft roe" or use the French *laitance*. Use only fresh milt, and remove the blue veins. Most all recipes begin by poaching the soft roe in white wine and lemon juice for about 2 to 5 minutes. From there, they can be sautéed in butter, with parsley and capers for garnish. They can be breaded and deep-fried. They can be mixed with mayonnaise and made into salads. Make a white sauce with the poaching liquor and serve atop soft roe on toast. Poached milt can be ground up and mixed with an equal amount of butter to make soft roe butter, to be used in broiling salmon steaks on toast, or in sauces. Blend up poached soft roe and mix it into quiches— if you're not a real man before you eat a milt quiche, you will be after. Don't take "I have a headache" for an answer. Try it anyway. Soft roe will become one of your favorites.

Hard roe—fish eggs—is a little easier to sell than soft roe. Roes can be salted as caviar, marinated in sake and soy sauce, sautéed, poached, mixed into canapés, served on sushi, served on kelp or hemlock, made into sauces, or simply eaten straight up. Edible roes come from sturgeon, herring, salmon, sea urchins, abalone, and shrimp.

Homemade Caviar

Several rules:

1. Use fresh, well-cared-for eggs, never more than a day old;
2. Use wood and plastic utensils, not metal;
3. Keep everything cold; and
4. Be gentle.

Remove the skein and membrane from the eggs. Try to separate the eggs, gently, perhaps using a ½-inch screen. Always try to remove any membrane. Carefully add the cold eggs to a cold brine mixture: for each cup of cold eggs, add ¼ cup of cold salt to a cup of cold water (remember rule No. 3). Gently stir the eggs with a wooden spoon. After 30 minutes, the eggs will grow firmer and the membranes will be easier to remove (along with broken eggs, for the ungentle among you). Drain the brine and rinse with cold water. Again, remove any membrane, drain, and keep refrigerated until ready to eat. It should keep for up to a month. Caviar should be served atop cream cheese and toast, with cooked eggs, or eaten by the spoonful, backed up with champagne.

Marinated Roe

Use herring roe on kelp or separated from skeins. Prepare two marinades: one for taste and one for preservation. For 8 hours, soak the roe in 6 parts mirin (substitute honey and sake or pale, dry sherry) and 4 parts soy sauce. Drain. Next, add roe to 7 parts rice vinegar and 3 parts soy sauce, which preserves it up to a month in the refrigerator. Try this approach with other roes. Serve it on sushi (vinegared) rice or seaweed.

Salmon roe, in skeins, can be rolled in flour or cornmeal and sautéed in butter or oil. They can also be lightly poached and then baked with onion, white sauce, and spices. Poached salmon eggs can be mixed with chopped, cooked chicken eggs and mayonnaise and added to salads. Poached salmon eggs can be added to white sauce and served on vegetables (especially freshly cooked spinach or peas) or omelets. Try other types of fish eggs in similar fashions. Poached herring roe can be mashed and mixed with scrambled eggs.

Herring roe is also excellent sautéed in butter, using lemon juice and capers. If your experiments don't quite taste right, add salsa; that can bring almost anything back to life. Use lots of lime juice, tomatoes, bell peppers, scallions, onions, red peppers, cayenne, jalapeño peppers, and cilantro.

So now you've been exposed to the ugly, sordid details. Far from disgusting, sex and violence go well with seafood. They may be the best place for it. Think of yourself as pushing the envelope of culinary decency. Enjoy them all now, before you-know-who tries to make them illegal.

Sexy Seafood Has the Power of Aphrodite

Aphrodite, the goddess of love, was born of the foam of the sea. About her, Homer said, ". . . she overcomes all mortal men and immortal gods with desire." Aphrodite's powers to arouse and excite have been bestowed upon all seafood, especially shellfish. Another goddess of love, Venus, raced about mythical waters astride a giant scallop shell at planting speeds. Later, Madame Du Barry, proficient in "la cuisine l'amour," based her aphrodisiacal recipes upon generous use of shrimp and other fish. If the great lovers of the world ascribe their powers to seafood, you may as well do likewise.

The following seafood recipes, two salads and two entrees, consist entirely of foods and spices known or supposedly endowed with the powers of Aphrodite. I've tried these out on Test Subjects, and some of their responses can be included. Finally, I've mentioned some tips on special aphrodisiacal foods and spices.

Both seafood salad recipes call for a vinaigrette: to 1 cup of olive oil, add ¼ cup of vinegar. Since plain vinegar is only mildly erotic, double your bets by using wine vinegar or tarragon vinegar. Or use both—it tastes better. One teaspoon of dijon mustard or fresh basil is optional. Blend these ingredients with a wire whisk or in a cocktail shaker.

Scallop-Stuffed Tomato

Chop up 1 cup of raw scallops and add enough vinaigrette to cover. Let this marinate while chilled for at least several hours, overnight if possible. Meanwhile, cut off the tops of 2 tomatoes and scoop out the innards. (Save the discards for the next recipe.) When ready to serve, mix 2 chopped green onions and a jigger of mayonnaise into the scallops. Fill the tomatoes with this mix, garnish with cilantro or parsley, and serve.

[Test Subject No. 1, a transplanted New Englander, pronounced this "fit to eat." Later, he confided to a friend that he'd actually noted "strange bodily sensations." You can't expect much more, I guess.]

Rice Seafood Salad

Ingredients for 4 servings:

Take 2 cups of cooked shrimp or crab, or both. Add 2 cups of cool, but cooked brown rice. Then add ½ cup each of chopped cucumbers, celery, tomato, and red onion. Throw in a teaspoon each of cilantro (or parsley) and tarragon. Toss well with 1 cup of the vinaigrette and serve well chilled.

[Test Subject No. 2, an enchanting sailor and avid skier, said she ate "too much" of this on a Sunday night and the next thing she remembered was Wednesday. She did recall the salad as being "vaguely delicious."]

Seductive Shrimp

In a large, hot, heavy skillet, add 2 ounces of olive oil, 2 chopped green onions, and 1 clove of minced garlic (be sure to see the hints on garlic toward the end of this chapter). Sauté not more than 1 minute. Now add 1 pound of shelled raw prawns or large shrimp. If you devein shrimp, use a knife to cut well past the vein, almost splitting the fat end of the shrimp. This way the cooked shrimp spreads open butterfly fashion. Sauté the shrimp quickly. When they've just turned pink, add ½ cup of sake or white wine. Simmer for 3 more minutes, not longer.

[Test Subject No. 3, a diminutive blonde fireball of Swedish stock, described the shrimp as "succulent."]

Ginger Snapper

Slice a pound of rockfish fillets into 1- or 2-inch slabs. Prepare 1 cup of marinade by adding equal amounts of sake and soy sauce, a chopped green onion, 1 teaspoon of honey, and 1 tablespoon of freshly grated ginger root. Marinate while chilled. After several hours, pour off the marinade and boil it for use as a dipping sauce. Add sesame oil to a hot skillet and sauté the rockfish for about 3 minutes on each side.

[Test Subject No. 4, a cautious and erudite soft-spoken type, at first denied any reaction. Upon reflection, No. 4 finally admitted to "the most vivid, graphic sexual dreams I've experienced in literally months."]

There are other recipes, but I'll save them for another time. Too much of this at one time can be harmful. Now for general comments and hints.

On garlic: Long recognized in both Asia and the West for its aphrodisiacal properties. Garlic eaters claim to be towers of strength, and vampires are not known as endearing lovers. Here are two garlic tricks. First, when frying, set aside a special jar of olive oil and dump in a handful of mashed garlic cloves. Olive oil itself also has stimulative powers. After a few days, the oil assumes a rich garlic flavor and the cloves don't dry out as they do on a refrigerator shelf. Replenish the oil as it's used, and replace the garlic cloves as needed. Second, avoid the tedium of daily peeling and chopping garlic cloves. Get several bulbs of garlic and remove the outer skins, roots, and stems. It's not necessary to peel each clove. Place the cloves in a blender and cover with olive oil. Blend at highest speed until the skins get pulverized. If sealed tightly and well refrigerated, this garlic paste should keep for some time.

On honey: Rich in minerals and nutrients, amino acids, and B-complex vitamins, honey has also been long regarded as a classic aphrodisiac. The virtues of bee pollen are also well known. The "honey" in "honeymoon" alludes to the necessary generous consumption of honey during that first intense month of marriage. And Sheikh Nefrazi recommended a hot broth of honey and onion juices, for one night only, in *The Perfumed Garden*. Whenever possible, substitute honey for sugar, which has no sensual effects. For two volumes of sugar, substitute one volume of honey.

On thyme: Supposedly the most potent of the erotic spices. Ancient writings warn against use of too much thyme.

On salt: Ordinary NaCl is not exciting, but sea salt is a different matter. And when available, clean seawater is recommended for cooking.

On other spices: Basil, cayenne, cinnamon, cloves, curry, dill, fennel, ginseng, mint, nutmeg, paprika, pepper, rosemary, and saffron can be added to those already mentioned in our recipes as being aphrodisiacs.

On teas: Mix black tea with ginseng tea (about a 4-to-1 ratio, respectively) and add any of the above spices for sexual sipping beverages.

On wine: As with other matters, in love there is danger with too much alcohol. One of the Bard's characters put it well: "It provokes the desire, but takes away the performance." Nevertheless, there is one famous concoction for those weekend morning pre-sail warm-up brunches. To a huge champagne glass, add a dollop of orange juice, a quartered strawberry, and fill to the top with a dry champagne.

Aphrodite's constitution would provide for the basic inalienable rights: life, love, and the pursuit of seafood. How can it go wrong? Fresh scallops, fish, and shrimp, clean, hearty vegetables, invigorating spices, and good company to share the fun of it all.

Toss them
quickly...

CHAPTER 20

SALADS FROM THE SEA

A hybrid meal, the warm seafood salad sits on middle ground, approaching the civilized notion of fire and cooking from one side, but avoiding the high heat that destroys nutrition and the delicate tastes of seafood on the other. Although the traditional "wilted" salad may not sound appetizing, you will find it surprisingly tasty. In this chapter, we adapt a few traditional wilted salad recipes by using healthier ingredients and adding seafood for a classier taste.

Traditionally, you pour sizzling bacon grease over lettuce to wilt it, and toss it with vinegar sweetened with sugar. Then you garnish it with crumbled bacon, hard-boiled egg slices, and wedges of tomato. Not bad, but nowhere good enough. Two healthy improvements are substituting unsaturated oils for bacon grease and honey for sugar.

Most people tear lettuce leaves rather than cut them with a knife. Lettuce leaves should be rinsed, dried with a towel, and crispened in the refrigerator for normal cold salads. Salad dressings normally consist of 3 parts oil to 1 part vinegar. Tomatoes should be placed stem down, thinly sliced vertically, and set aside to drain the juices and seeds. Add tomatoes as garnish after tossing the salad.

Most cookbooks call for leaf-type lettuce in wilted recipes. Romaine and iceberg lettuces do not give up their crispness easily and resist wilting. Butterleaf lettuce is a fine, delicate candidate. Fresh spinach excels in wilted salad recipes. Adventurous gathering types can harvest small dandelion greens.

The hot oil method is the traditional method wherein you pour hot oil into a bowl of green leaves and toss them quickly. I suggest olive oil in one recipe, but you must not let olive oil be too hot for too long. Do not let the oil emit blue smoke or even let it get near that temperature.

The hot skillet method resembles a quickie stir-fry where the salad ingredients are added to a hot skillet and briefly sautéed. The hot skillet method allows seafood to be cooked first, leaving the tasty seafood juices to become part of the warm salad "dressing." Now for some recipes.

Ginger Soy Seafood Salad

Use the hot wok method for this one. If you have no wok, use a large skillet. I have suggested certain seafoods, but feel free to experiment with any other combinations.

Ingredients for 4 servings:

2 ounces peanut oil
4 ounces scallops, bite-sized chunks
4 ounces shrimp, peeled
4 ounces halibut chunks
4 ounces thick squid steak, pounded, cut into strips
1 head leaf lettuce, torn into shreds
1 cucumber, partly peeled and sliced
l bunch green onions, chopped
1 ounce ginger root, grated
1 ounce rice wine vinegar
1 teaspoon soy sauce
1 tomato, sliced

In a hot wok, add the oil and sauté the scallops, shrimp, and halibut for about 5 minutes. Then add the squid, which cooks much faster, and cook for 1 to 2 minutes. Add all the remaining ingredients, except the tomato, and toss the salad in the wok for 1 to 2 minutes more until the lettuce shows the first signs of wilting. Remove from the heat and serve quickly. Add the tomato slices as garnish.

THE ID AND THE SQUID

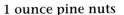

Italian Wilted Salad

Use the hot oil method for this one. The original recipe calls for prosciutto, a smoked, dry Italian ham, thinly sliced. I substitute smoked salmon, the hot-smoked, dry variety. The recipe also requires fresh basil leaves, sometimes a problem to find. For a substitute, use fresh or frozen pesto sauce. If you can only find dried basil, forget this recipe.

Ingredients for 4 servings:

1 ounce pine nuts
6 ounces smoked salmon, in small pieces
2 ounces olive oil, cooking grade
2 cloves garlic, smashed flat and
    chopped
2 large bunches fresh spinach,
    rinsed and torn
1 large bunch fresh basil leaves
1 tablespoon red wine vinegar
2 ounces Parmesan cheese,
    grated
Freshly ground black pepper
    to taste

In a medium-hot skillet with a trace of oil, toast the pine nuts for a few moments. Remove them and add the smoked salmon, just to warm it. Remove the salmon, add the oil and garlic, and quickly heat to sizzling. Meanwhile, have the spinach and basil leaves ready in the serving bowl. Pour the hot oil over the leaves and quickly toss them. Heat the vinegar in the skillet, pour the vinegar over the leaves, and toss quickly again. Then toss in the salmon, pine nuts, and Parmesan cheese. Add pepper to taste.

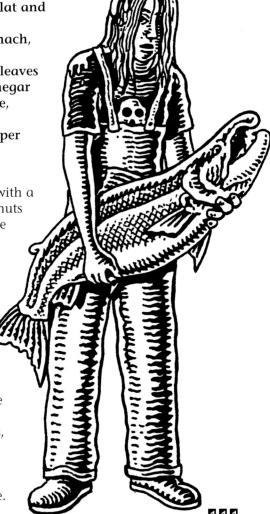

Flaming Shrimp Salad

Ingredients for 4 servings:

4 ounces peanut oil
1 cup shrimp, peeled
2 large bunches spinach, rinsed and torn
1 can mandarin orange slices
Juice of 1 lemon
1 ounce white wine vinegar
2 ounces triple sec

In a hot skillet with a long handle, add the oil and shrimp. Fry the shrimp until done and place them in a bowl with the spinach leaves and orange slices. Leave as much of the oil in the skillet as possible. Reheat the oil, add to the spinach, and toss. Add the lemon juice and vinegar to the skillet; heat to boiling. Add to the spinach and toss.

Now heat the triple sec in the skillet, carefully ignite the liqueur, and pour the flaming liquid over the salad. Serve with a flourish and a fire extinguisher.

Intertidal Vegetables

Behold the intrepid fisherman. He's caught more seaweed than salmon. He mutters clichés: "Well, I caught the salad." He curses his luck and flings overboard his only edible foodstuff, returning to port in folly, empty-handed and hungry. He should have kept those greens because they're expeditious and nutritious. Packed with more vitamins than liver, seaweed has been a mainstay in far-flung cultures throughout the world, from Scotland to Baja, from Tokyo to Kake, Alaska. The Pacific Northwest abounds with a wealth of tasty intertidal vegetables. It's about time we appreciated them more.

Seaweeds have been part of our diets for centuries. In early England they were the primary source of iodine. Kelp fertilized farmlands, and kelp ash formed soap. Natives of the Kamchatka Peninsula fermented their seaweed to make an alcoholic brew. North American Indians thought the use of salt abhorrent but used dried seaweed as a source of organic seasoning. Japanese algae farmers have been growing seaweed crops since the 1700s. The Seri Indians of the Baja ground dried eelgrass into flour and made a staple porridge, eaten daily. Polynesians used 75 different types of seaweed. Early written records from Iceland and China mention seaweed as important factors in 800 B.C. life.

The rocky shorelines from Washington through Alaska support luxurious growths of seven common edible seaweeds. In fact, it's hard to find an inedible seaweed. Seaweeds are unaffected by red tides, which are microscopic algae. Thus, abalone and urchins that graze upon macroscopic algae—seaweed—are also not affected. Before we go much further, look at the names and descriptions of the seven various types of seaweed in the chart.

Scientific Name	European Name	Japanese Name	Folk Name	Nutrition
Alaria	bladderlochs	wakame	wing kelp edible kelp kelp	Vitamins B-6 and K; Iodine
Fucus	bladderwrack	n.a.	rockweed popweed	Vitamin C (early fall); Vitamin A (summer); Iodine
Laminaria	tangle	kombu	sugar wrack oarweed	Vitamin C (late spring); Sugars in summer; Iodine; Protein
Nereocystis	(found only in NW Pacific)	n.a.	bullwhip kelp	Iodine
Palmaria (formerly Rhodymonia)	dulse	darusu	red kale raa-ts (Tlingit)	Vitamin A (summer); Vitamin C (fall); Protein; Fat; Iodine; Phosphorus, one of the best
Porphyra	laver slook	nori	laver	Vitamin C; Protein
Ulva	lettuce laver green laver	aosa	sea lettuce	Vitamin C (late spring); Iron; Protein; Iodine

Illustrations © Roxanne Turner

The references to nutrition in the chart only mention exceptional values. Let's continue to talk about nutrition. Since seaweeds have no active roots, all nutrients transfer through the leaves. Seaweeds are rich in vitamins and minerals. The list would be too long to cover in detail, but here are some examples.

- Vitamin A: laver contains more than chicken eggs or liver.
- Vitamin B: most green algaes contain more B-12 than liver and compare to that of most fruits and vegetables.
- Vitamin C: laver, sea lettuce, and kelp contain as much as lemons.
- Iodine: a few grams of dried seaweed contain enough; it's possible to overdose on iodine with seaweed, especially popweed.
- Iron: compares with whole wheat.
- Calcium: a tablespoon of dried seaweed contains as much as a glass of milk.
- Protein: 25 percent of the dry weight, easily digested.
- Carbohydrate: compares to oats.

Some seaweeds are used as gelatins. When given the choice between animal gelatins (made from the hooves and cartilage of cattle) and the seaweed gelatins known as algins or carrageenans, go vegetarian.

A few words on collecting and preserving seaweeds. When possible, leave the holdfast and some stipe. The regeneration is much faster that way—seaweed has some of the fastest growth rates of all plants. The ends and edges of the fronds are the oldest parts, so trim the ends and keep the part of the frond closest to the midrib, if any. Some people rinse seaweed in fresh water and some in salt water. Just make sure there's no sand or snails left. Do not rinse off the sticky mucilage from the surface. This gelatinous substance contains the proteins and sugars that make seaweed especially nutritious. Open-air drying is the best preservation. Clam juice can be dripped on dried seaweed and then re-dried for excellent results. To restore dried seaweed, simply place it in cold water for a few minutes. Kelp and sugar wrack do not freeze well but are wonderful slightly smoked. Other seaweed can be frozen, with or without being blanched.

The easiest way to get seaweed is to eat it raw. All tastes good; some tastes excellent. My favorite is sugar wrack, which contains a sugar alcohol, mannitol. Its full scientific name—*Laminaria saccharina*—also betrays its sweetness. Chopped raw seaweed of any variety enhances salads. Think of it for sandwiches.

Salt Substitute

As seasoning, seaweed is great. Simply crumble sheets of store-bought nori and use it like salt. For foragers, collect sea lettuce or laver from the beach and sun-dry it. Toast the dried seaweed several inches over an open flame for just a few seconds. Then crumble as above. Use it in popcorn, adding dried seaweed just as the corn begins to pop. It's also tops in salads and soups.

Bladderwrack Tea

In beverages, seaweed works well. Bladderwrack tea is sold in health food stores. It's said to clean out arteries, aid circulation, and help organ functions. It's also known as "slimming tea" because iodine stimulates thyroid functions to regulate metabolism and thus weight loss. Gather some popweed and remove the hard stipe. Wash well in cold, fresh water. Chop the fronds coarsely and open-air dry them. Then seal in a jar for later use: 1 to 2 teaspoons per cup of boiling water.

Hot Dulse Toddy / Kelp Bloody Mary

Try a Hot Dulse Toddy to cure what ails you. Take a handful of fresh or rehydrated dulse and boil it for 20 minutes. Pour a cup of the dulse tea through a strainer, add the juice of a lime, honey to taste, and a jigger of tequila or rum. To prevent what might ail you tomorrow, try the Kelp Bloody Mary. Take a handful of rehydrated store-bought wakame or fresh alaria fronds and blend them into a quart of tomato juice. Add the juice of 2 limes, crumbled nori (or equivalent), and pepperings (4 to 8 ounces of vodka is optional).

Seaweed Soups

About soups. Most store-bought instant miso soups already have kelp (as wakame) and laver (as nori) in them, as do the store-bought seaweed ramens. The seaweed books are full of soup recipes, European and Asian. Any of the common seaweeds (except bullwhip kelp and rockweed) will glorify most soups without mishap. An egg-flower breakfast soup starts the day quickly. Beat an egg with a small amount of olive oil. Add it to boiling water, and remove from heat while stirring. Add a handful of fresh or rehydrated seaweed. Sea lettuce or laver works well, but so do kelp, dulse, and sugar wrack.

Another soup uses the gelatinous compounds from seaweeds as well as the seaweed itself. Boil briefly 3 cups of tomato juice with ¼ cup of agar flakes. Remove from the heat, cool slightly, and add poached salmon flakes, lemon juice, horseradish, watercress, chopped onions, cucumber slices, and so forth. Add crumbled nori or chopped kelp fronds for more seaweed flavor. Chill for several hours in the refrigerator. This forms a jelly-like aspic with a bit of zing to it.

Seaweed Beach Barbecue

On the beach, steam and barbecue using seaweed. The greatest contribution from rockweed is in steaming fish and clams. Pack the bottom of a huge kettle with 6 or 8 inches of rinsed rockweed. Place salmon steaks or chunks or clams atop the rockweed and add another 6 to 8 inches to cover. Add several inches of fresh water and steam until done. Save the broth at the bottom and use it for sauces. The same principle can be applied to open fires if seawater is added frequently so as to keep the steam up and prevent the coals from incinerating the rockweed. Both ways, the rockweed imparts a delicate taste to the fish. Try it once and you'll do it often.

Beach baked salmon benefit from large fronds of kelp. Wrap a whole gutted salmon in several layers of kelp fronds and then in aluminum foil. In a well-along fire (coals only—remove burning logs), bury the wrapped fish in coals and then cover the coals with several inches of earth. After several hours, remove the fish and unwrap the foil. Chunk up the salmon with kelp wrapping; serve.

Just Fried

Fried seaweed. From my view, the best seaweed is dried and fried. Sea lettuce, kelp, dulse, laver, and sugar wrack excel if just dropped into hot olive oil for less than a second per side. Coated with beaten egg, these seaweeds taste even better. And tempura style is fantastic. If you're having difficulty with people overcoming their reluctance to try seaweed (the "yuk"ers), give them fried seaweed. Brushing these seaweeds with oil and toasting them in an oven produces similar results.

Another fried treat: wrap finger-sized chunks of salmon with sheets of nori, dip into beaten egg, dust with flour, and fry in hot olive oil. Soy sauce on the side.

So the next time you hook some seaweed or haul in an anchor-full of kelp, consider your good fortune. It's more nutritious and more tasty than an anchor-full of liver and now you know how to cook it. If you're gonna be intrepid, you gotta act intrepid. You can now say "I've caught the salad" and have it mean something.

Stalking the Beachside Salad

The situation: several days out of port, anchored in a cove, you begin to crave a fresh green salad. Your body senses the onset of scurvy. You peer into your icebox—your lettuce has turned into a dense, peatlike substance, there is a hint of movement of a new form of primordial life. Hopes for a salad vanish.

Despair not. A quick skiff ride to shore and you can harvest a natural crop of salad fixings to spice up any meal. The beaches of Alaska abound with half a dozen common types of delicious, green plants that can be used as salad, soup, vegetables, beverages, and garnishes. This section will tell you how to identify and prepare them.

These plants can be easily identified and grow right on the high-tide region. All can be cooked by boiling and, as such, can rank right in there with the best store-bought produce. The secret is to cook them quickly, about half the time of garden-variety garden vegetables. Another secret: do not overeat. These wild plants are rich in vitamins and nutrients—too rich in comparison to the wimpy cultivated crops that we're accustomed to. If you eat too much of any wild plant, your body is going to reject it.

Goosetongue

Also known as seaside plantain, this common perennial is related to the common lawn plant, which is tough and fibrous compared to its tender beachside cousin. Goosetongue grows everywhere, even in the craggiest rocky sea bluffs. The narrow, brittle gray-green leaves, 4 to 10 inches long, grow in a bunch directly from the root mass. The flowers crowd densely on the end of a leafless spike, which projects above the leaves. Do not confuse goosetongue with arrowgrass, which has narrower and rounder leaves.

Goosetongue can be frozen or canned. Use it fresh in salads or cooked like green beans. Serve with hollandaise sauce. I like to can it with small chunks of bacon. Also try goosetongue stir-fried in olive oil and garlic.

Sourdock

Also known as wild spinach and Arctic dock, this tart perennial is related to the sheep sorrel of Europe, where the French grow it on purpose in gardens. A large variety of this plant, from the buckwheat family, can be found, but the most common Alaska version grows up to 4 feet tall. The erect stem is reddish-purple. There's usually a big bunch of leaves at the base, roughly heart-shaped, up to 10 inches long. The leaves on the tall stem are smaller and alternate on each side as they go up. The top half of the mature stem is a slender cluster of tiny green or green-purple flowers.

Sourdock can be used in every course, from salad to dessert. The sour leaves go well in a sandwich, taking the place of relish or pickles. Add a cup of sourdock leaves for each potato in a potato soup. Place sourdock in a blender and make a puree of it. Simmer 2 cups of puree in a saucepan with 1 ounce of butter for 10 minutes. Add 2 ounces of cream and stir until hot and blended. Serve hot or cold. Chopped leaves make a garnish for fish or crab and can be mixed into potato salad. Boil some sourdock in water for a lemonade. Use sourdock like rhubarb for a dessert.

Wild Celery and Beach Parsley

Three types of Alaska seaside plants are called wild celery: seaside angelica, sea lovage, and cow parsnip. The wild celeries are of the parsley family, but so is the poison water hemlock. Water hemlock resembles angelica and cow parsnip but not beach parsley. My advice: stick with beach parsley. The identification is easy and the others aren't that great for flavor and require too much work and caution in preparation.

Beach parsley grows low to the ground just above the intertidal area. Identify it by its three stems, each stem with three leaves. Chop it up for a parsley substitute, steam it or can it as a vegetable, or use it in salads and soups. Some of the best meals I've ever cooked have used beach parsley.

Scurvy Grass

Also known as spoonwort, scurvy grass cured many of the early explorers of their dreaded nemesis caused by vitamin C deficiency. Captain Cook often came ashore to collect scurvy grass, which grows in the circumpolar regions into the high Arctic. It's a member of the mustard family and is related to cress, cabbage, radishes, and the like. The fleshy, veinless leaves are simple and small, with a spoon-like shape, an inch across. Like all members of the mustard family, the flowers are small with six stamens and four white petals arranged in a cross. It's a small plant less than a foot high.

Probably the tastiest of all wild greens, scurvy grass can be mixed into salads or carefully boiled like other greens, but think of it as watercress. On rye bread, spread cream cheese and a thick layer of scurvy grass leaves. Or use it as a garnish on cold poached salmon. Mix it in with sour cream for baked potatoes.

Beach Greens

Also known as Eskimo kraut, seabeach sandwort, and sea chickweed, beach greens also cured scurvy in the early days of Arctic exploration, as well as providing a good source of vitamin A. This plant grows as a low, sprawling mat on sandy beaches. The fleshy, succulent leaves are paired opposite each other on the stem. The tiny flowers are greenish-white with five petals.

Early in the season, the leaves can be eaten raw or in salads. They make a good garnish for fish. Beach greens can also be made into a sauerkraut. And, as always, they can be boiled.

Silverweed

Also known as wild sweet potato, silverweed produces runners like strawberries. The stems are up to 9 inches long and often lie on the ground. On each stem, there are many small sharply toothed leaflets, shiny smooth on top and white silky underneath. The flowers are large, yellow, and have five petals, a very pretty plant.

It's the roots of the silverweed that are eaten raw, boiled, or roasted. Treat them like small potatoes.

Other Edibles

Both spruce and hemlock needles make a good tea, also alluded to as scurvy cures by the early Alaska explorers Cook and Vancouver. Simply pour boiling water over them, steep for a few minutes, decant, and serve. The inner bark of hemlock and willow provides a good energy source and is surprisingly tasty. Strip it out and dry it. The bulbs of the chocolate lily, found in coastal marshes, make good eating when dried out and boiled. The fresh, young leaves of fireweed, often found near the high-tide line of beaches, make good green vegetables also.

Whether you're a survivalist, a nuts-among-the-berries type, shipwrecked, or a fisherman just hungry for a fresh salad, it pays to know the beachside marketplace. The green plants just above the high-tide line taste just as good as any other—and the price is right. And one of the best ways to appreciate Nature is by eating it.

Make your
     own choices
about the
       eyeballs.

CHAPTER 21

IF FISH EYES OFFEND THEE, PLUCK THEM FROM THY SOUP

The omega-3 fish oils have forced rethinking of heart disease and given new meaning for fish-head soup. Again, medical studies and nutrition experts advance another theory of fish food benefits. Here we have recipes for fish-head soup intended to capture and enhance the fish oils, using their flavors and nutrition.

The fish oil revelations come to us thanks to studies of Greenland Eskimos, who, despite their high-fat, high-cholesterol diet, showed mysteriously few signs of heart disease. Lab studies confirmed that heavy fish oil diets, using salmon-rich feeding trials, result in much improved blood and body conditions. Researchers now think that fish oils benefit inflammatory diseases, such as arthritis, and eases blood vessel-related ailments, such as migraine headaches.

Tests show the oil contents of typical fish samples to be, based on a 4-ounce serving: salmon, 2.3 to 3.6 grams; mackerel, 1.8 to 2.6 grams; herring, 1.2 to 2.7 grams; and albacore, about 2.6 grams.

The following recipes are intended for salmon, sablefish, tuna, and other oily fish.

Generic Fish Oil Stock

Here's a wonderful fish soup made from things people normally discard. I think of this as a free meal. Fish oils are concentrated in certain areas of fish: in the head, near the skin, and along the belly. Take whatever fish heads, tails, and bellystrips you can find and boil them for 30 minutes or so. Use ample water in a large cauldron. Make sure the fish heads are well cleaned of the gill tissue and the like. If you can find a backbone, add it also. Remove the heads, bones, and strips from the pot, pick the meat away from the skin, bone, and gristly parts, and save the meat. Make your own choices about the eyeballs.

Now add to the simmering pot certain vegetable parts that you've been saving in the refrigerator: onion skins, carrot peelings, outer leaves of leeks or green onions, broccoli stems, tough celery stalks, parsley stems and so forth. Add a few spices, thyme, garlic, a bay leaf. Continue to simmer for another half hour. Then strain or remove the limp vegetable remains.

Now you have options. You can toss the fish meat back in and call it soup. If you wish, the soup can be fortified with more vegetables, such as onions, celery, carrots, peas, cabbage, or whatever is at hand. If more fortification is needed, add a couple of cans of clams, including juice.

And you can freeze the stock and meat and use it to make soup for future meals. It's much preferable to freeze the stock, which retains flavors well, rather than to freeze the fish heads and other trimmings.

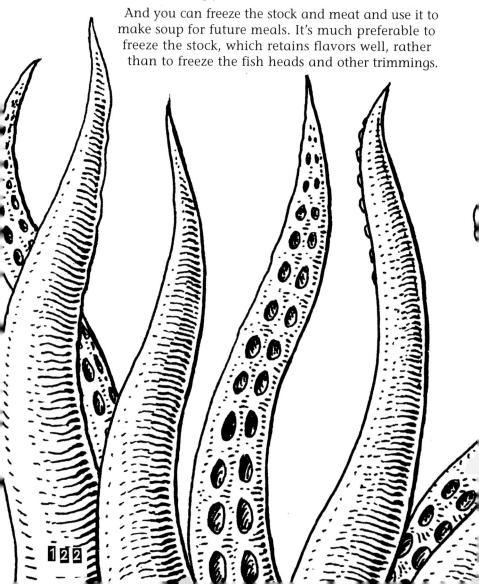

Soup d' Poisson

In a large cast-iron kettle, place 2 chopped onions and 1 chopped leek. Add 2 jiggers of green olive oil and sauté the onions and leeks until they're just soft and barely transparent. Add 6 mashed garlic cloves and 3 chopped tomatoes. For spices, add a bunch of chopped parsley, a sprig of thyme, a bay leaf, and 1 tablespoon of fennel seeds. Simmer for another 5 minutes.

Add a fifth of Generic Fish Oil Stock and a pint of white wine and bring to a slow boil. Add inch-sized chunks of the fish you wish to cook—I suggest halibut, snapper, or salmon. Simmer for no more than 10 minutes.

Meanwhile in another pot, add a fifth of fish stock and either a pinch of saffron or 1 teaspoon of turmeric. Peel 4 potatoes and slice them into ½-inch rounds. Add them to the pot and boil for 10 minutes or less. When the potatoes are barely cooked and still waxy looking, remove the pot from the heat and set it aside.

Strain and remove about half the chunky parts from the soup. Then either rub them through a sieve or pulverize them in a food processor. Return them to the soup and mix it up.

At serving time, place the sliced potatoes in the bottom of wide soup dishes. Pour on the soup and serve with grated Parmesan or Romano cheese.

The health benefits claimed for fish oils can be found in no other oils or sources. It seems as though the folklore about the health attributes of fish ring truer the more we learn and research. The experts advise eating oily fish at least twice a week. Much better to cook with these recipes than to take cod liver oil from the bottle.

Fish Oil Sauce

In addition to the reduced white wine sauce described earlier, here's another sauce that uses the fish oils. For 2 cups of sauce, mix 1 tablespoon of olive oil with 1 tablespoon of flour in a hot saucepan. Let this warm and bubble. Slowly add, stirring constantly, 1 cup of our fish stock. Try to skim and concentrate the fish oil from the stock to add to the sauce. Also add ½ cup of cream. When this thickens and looks about right, add ½ cup of the fish pieces picked and saved from the stock making, described above. Serve atop pasta or steamed vegetables. Garnish with sliced hard-boiled egg and parsley sprigs.

Canned Fish Spaghetti Sauce

The canning process also captures fish oils, especially if the skin and bones are included. The health advantages for fish bones also include their calcium contribution to prevent osteoporosis, the brittle bone disease of older folks. Be sure to save the liquids in the can for their oil content.

Chop 1 large onion, a handful of mushrooms, and several cloves of garlic. In a large skillet, sauté these in olive oil until the onion pieces become transparent. Add a couple of chopped tomatoes and a can of tomato sauce, and spice with basil. Also add the juices and oils from the canned fish. Let this simmer until the tomato chunks are cooked. Finally add the canned fish, with chunks broken into smaller flakes, and simmer a few minutes longer to warm up the fish. Serve atop pasta, with a garnish of chopped green and black olives.

Not-Quite-Instant Soup

A desperate situation: you're at the supermarket to fetch Alaska seafood fixings for a gourmet meal. Now, without inspiration and with an empty market basket, you're passing the instant soup shelves. What luck. You remember reading this chapter that tells you how, without inspiration or recipes, you can save the day. This is a nine-step process, but it makes sense.

Step one: Pick an instant soup mix of some sort of vegetable base. A chicken- or beef-based soup will not work in this scheme that adapts itself to added seafood.

Step two: Go to the fresh fish section of the supermarket and buy the fish that goes with the soup. For each type of vegetable soup base, there corresponds a type of seafood. For example, pea soup goes with salmon. Leek or potato soup goes with halibut, oysters, or clams. Asparagus soup goes with shrimp. Bean soup goes with smoked black cod. Tomato soup goes with cod or snapper. Mushroom soup goes with crab or oysters. Broccoli also goes with crab. And so on.

Step three: Read the list of ingredients on the instant soup package. Go to the produce section of the supermarket and buy some fresh produce that corresponds to the list of dehydrated ingredients. For example, the instant split pea soup package lists dehydrated onions and carrots.

Step four: Make a soup stock from the trimmings of the fresh produce and seafood. On our example of split pea soup, take the ends and peeled outer skins of the onions and carrots along with the bones of the salmon, and boil them in a quart or so of water. Add more spices (again, for inspiration, read the ingredient list on the package) and wine. Remove the trimmings and bones after 10 or 15 minutes.

Step five: Follow the instructions on the soup mix package. Usually, that means boiling the ingredients in water. Except, in this case, use the stock from step four instead of water.

Step six: Chop and sauté the fresh produce. Use olive oil for the best flavor, but use medium, never high, heat. And sauté lightly, just to soften the edges.

Step seven: Chop the seafood, salmon in this case, into chunks about 1 inch in thickness.

Step eight: Just 10 minutes before the soup mix instructions say the soup is finished cooking, add the sautéed vegetables and the chopped seafood. If milk or powdered milk is to be added, do it at this time or later, so as not to burn the milk.

Step nine: Garnish with parsley, bread crumbs, Parmesan cheese, yogurt, sour cream, croutons, and so forth. Serve with wine.

This approach to gourmet seafood soup has several advantages other than not having to remember any recipes. The soup doesn't have to be overcooked to bring out the flavor of the ingredients, since the dried flavorings and the stock do that much. This means the vegetable ingredients are crunchy and tasty and the seafood ingredients are never overcooked.

"Surely you
don't eat them?"
I asked.

CHAPTER 22

DUCKS OF THE SEA, FIRE OF THE EARTH

My hunting buddy Bob confessed to shooting sea ducks.

"Surely you don't mean those fishy-tasting, black diving ducks," I said. "Not those skunkheads?"

"Sure do," said Bob. "There's more sport to it than you'd figure. Big sea ducks like skunkheads deceive you with their speed. Gotta lead them according to how fast they swim. You can judge by the size of their wakes."

"Surely you don't eat them?" I asked.

"Sure do," said Bob, with a twisted, strange gleam in his eye. "I got a secret recipe—Chinese. It purifies the fishy taste of sea ducks."

Bob's got a Ph.D. in ecology. Maybe he knows something. So I tried his secret recipe and I'm here to tell you it works.

Bob's Secret: Ginger

Chinese regard ginger as more than medicine, as more than food. Ginger replenishes the energy of life, it empowers the soul, it allows communication with the spirits. So there's a lot more to ginger than purifying the fishy taste of sea ducks.

Chinese cooks balance the five basic flavors like musicians harmonize instruments. For example, recall hot and sour soup. The "hot" or pungent flavor, from ginger, balances the sour flavor. Take a slice of ginger and chew it for a minute. You'll know the meaning of pungent. Your stomach will warm, and sweat will come to your brow. You've discovered the "Fire of the Earth."

Chinese sailors chew ginger to prevent seasickness and scurvy. Ginger has relieved morning sickness and nausea at large. Ancient and classic texts cited ginger's aphrodisiac powers, and some early herbalists gave warnings on their prescriptions for ginger's lusty side effects. Ginger also aids the digestive tract and

is said to cure flatulence. These latter medicinal qualities may have explained the twisted, strange gleam in Bob's eye.

Early Chinese writings mention ginger's use to cure and preserve venison, to eliminate the stench of raw flesh. Chinese fishmongers still add slices of ginger and green onions in packages of fish sales to remove even the slightest odors. Most all Chinese duck and goose recipes use ginger to counteract the game taste.

A Recipe: Thai Duck

This dish generates several incredible tastes and various bodily reactions. One portion can taste distinctly different from the last. Be sure to have plenty of cold beer and white wine handy. Ginger plays a role both to purify the fishy tastes of the sea duck in the marinade and to punctuate the dish itself.

To purify the duck, take 4 breasts and slice them along the grain in long, pencil-width sections. Other duck parts should be cut likewise. Take a good-sized handful of freshly grated ginger and massage it into the duck pieces. Place it all in a bowl, add a tumbler of sake, and marinate it in the refrigerator for a couple of hours. If you're out of sake, use dry white wine. After removing the duck pieces from the marinade, sauté them in peanut oil. Use a wok if you have one; otherwise use a cast-iron frying pan.

For the dish, slice peeled ginger lengthwise along its grain, then cut into matchstick-sized slivers. Place a handful of ginger slivers in a large serving bowl, then add 2 handfuls of cilantro, 1 handful of fresh basil leaves, 1 bunch of parsley, and 1 handful of fresh mint leaves, all coarsely chopped. Toss in handfuls of bean sprouts, chopped green onions, and sliced mushrooms. Cut up a lime into many thin slices and toss that in as well. Now, according to your ability to withstand pain, add as many chopped hot red chile peppers as you can tolerate.

Add the sautéed duck to the serving bowl with the juice of a freshly squeezed lime and a little olive oil. Toss it well. Before serving, make a big fuss about the aromas. Make everyone smell it before tasting.

For options, add Asian wheat noodles, slices of lemon grass, sautéed raw peanuts, garlic cloves, honey, fish sauce, sesame oil, rice vinegar, or, my favorite, sake. This should serve 4 to 6 people.

Epilogue

So now there are two of us out there shooting sea ducks. We both have twisted, strange gleams in our eyes, but we've shared our ancient secrets of the Chinese duck chefs. The Fire of the Earth has brought us enough understanding of harmony to bring terror to the rafts of skunkheads swimming, even flying sometimes.

I surprised Roxanne
by exclaiming,
"Wow, hooters!"

CHAPTER 23
HOOTERS AND BEER

On my first date with Roxanne, we went on a spring picnic to North Douglas Island in Southeast Alaska. Roxanne was a bit edgy to be alone in the woods with someone she barely knew, but hey, you gotta take risks, right? She had been warned that I was weird, but she didn't know about my obsession with hooters. Or, let's say, what Roxanne knew about hooters had nothing to do with the male Blue Grouse *(Dendragapus obscurus)*, which was in mating season on North Douglas.

So I heard the mating call of some bull hooters off in the distance. I surprised Roxanne by exclaiming, "Wow, hooters!" She said, "Nice weather," and eyed the distance to the car, wondering if she could get to the door before I could.

I saw the fear in her eyes and said, "No really, I'm serious, it's a bird. Listen . . . please." And I gave her my best imitation of a hooter, but no hooters hooted in response.

Roxanne now knew that her worst nightmares were coming true. She edged toward the car, whistling. A hooter hooted, but she couldn't hear it for her whistling. I begged her to listen. I gave another imitation of a hooter, this time blowing over the top of an empty Heineken beer bottle for better sound effects.

At last, Roxanne rolled the window down a crack and heard a hooter hooting. The picnic was saved. A week later, we went hooter hunting. The males will hoot, usually well-camouflaged high in the canopy of Sitka spruce trees, despite being repeatedly shot at. Not smart. We used these recipes. If you can't find hooter meat, pheasant is a poor substitute and chicken is only for practice.

Van's Secret Sherry Hooters

Most hooter hunters are secretive. When I hunt with Van, he blindfolds me on the trip to the site and makes me hike in without my glasses. He gave me this recipe on the condition that I blindfold my guests while I cook it, and then I have to eat the recipe after I use it.

Marinate the hooter breasts in olive oil, white vinegar, and white wine. Then sear the breasts in a skillet using butter. Remove the breasts and deglaze the skillet with sherry. Add cream, rosemary, pepper, and paprika. Add the breasts and simmer for a while. Serve with rice and asparagus.

Art's Secret Gibson Grouse

Sear hooter breasts and sliced mushrooms in a skillet with olive oil and butter. Deglaze the skillet with 4 ounces of gin, add a splash of vermouth, and a handful of pearl onions. Add dried morels. Simmer for 1 hour, adding water as necessary. Add cream and butter and juniper berries if available and serve with martinis.

Tracey's Secret Bluetooth Hooters

This recipe turns your teeth blue, but not for too long. Hooters eat blueberries in the summer, and the locals say hooters get drunk on fermented blueberries in the fall. This only partly explains the stuporous behavior of hooters: that of appearing besotted year-round. Mix up 1 ounce of dijon mustard and ½ cup apricot jam, and spread the mix over the breasts. Brown the hooter breasts in a skillet with butter. After the breasts have been turned once, add a handful of blueberries to the breasts in the skillet. Heat for a short while and remove breasts and berries. Then add 2 ounces of white wine vinegar to the skillet and simmer until the sauce is reduced by half. Return the breasts to the skillet and serve.

Randy's Secret Spruce Tea Hooters

Since the main winter diet for hooters is spruce needles, this recipe uses spruce needle tea, rich in vitamin C. You make spruce needle tea by collecting fresh green tips of spruce boughs in spring. Crush the tips with a rolling pin, mash them into a cup, and cover with boiling water.

Make a roux: add equal parts butter and flour to a skillet, stirring constantly over medium-low heat until it turns a leather-brown color, about 15 minutes. Roux can be kept refrigerated for weeks.

Marinate the hooter breasts in 1 cup of spruce needle tea, a jigger of honey, and a grated chunk of ginger. Drain and dry the breasts and save the marinade. Sauté the breasts in a skillet with smoking-hot olive oil. Remove the breasts and deglaze the skillet with 4 ounces of sake. Caution: Sake may catch fire and flare up, which can be entertaining with proper planning. Use dry sherry if you don't have sake. Add 1 ounce of roux and then 1 cup of marinade, letting it thicken into a sauce. Serve the sauce on the breasts over wild rice.

Smooth Sailing with Spruce Beer

Captain Cook was the Euell Gibbons of his day. Obsessed with finding the cure for scurvy, Captain Cook stopped often to go ashore stalking wild undiscovered plants and herbs. His crews had mixed feelings about some of Cook's concoctions. But when they explored the Pacific Northwest in 1778, the records showed a gluttonous consumption of a "spruce beer," said to be high in vitamin C. Later in this, Cook's third and fatal voyage, the log of the *Resolution* read that spruce beer removed the deadly "seeds of scurvy" while in the windswept Aleutians. In earlier voyages, Cook referred to spruce beer in the Queen Charlottes in February 1777 and in New Zealand in March 1773.

George Vancouver was a junior officer during Cook's expeditions. He remembered spruce beer well later in his own travels. In 1794, Captain Vancouver ended his three-year exploration in aptly named Port Conclusion with a spruce beer celebration. The log of the *Discovery* read, "grog in abundance was passed." Captain Vancouver had tried a hemlock beer earlier and "this was found to make a very palatable and equally salubrious beverage."

Cook's basic spruce beer ingredients—molasses and spruce—kept well without spoiling and, with the British palate accustomed to stout ales, its resemblance to turpentine mattered little. Captain Vancouver's version added ginger to the recipe. I've tried several substitutions and additions. The results have ranged from ales to champagnes. Spruce beer brews easily and quickly, so you may want to store some basic ingredients for those long voyages when one could run out of garden-variety beer.

Substituting honey for molasses shifts the taste from stout ale to lighter beer. Should you go for the stout, be sure to use unsulfured molasses. There are several grades of molasses for some variety in stoutness. Adding lime juice to the honey version improves the anti-scurvy properties. It also makes the brew more resemble a dry champagne, especially if you omit the spruce needles. You can see the potential for experimentation, so keep careful records.

My recipes are all based upon the greatest boon to home brewers in recent years—Grolsch beer. A German import with a snap-top bottle, it eliminates the need for a capping machine. My favorite tavern saves their empties for me. At 16 ounces each, 8 bottles make a gallon, and the recipes that follow are for 1-gallon batches.

Cleanliness and boiling water reduce your chances for an accidental batch of vinegar. Begin by washing the Grolsch bottles in hot, soapy water. Rinse well with hot water, fill to the top with boiling water, and cap until ready to refill.

Next, finely grate 2 ounces of ginger root into a small pan of water. Boil the mixture for 10 minutes or so. Meanwhile, wash a gallon container of some sort and rinse it with boiling water. Pour the boiled ginger mixture through a fine sieve into the gallon container. Discard the root pulp. Take 1 cup of the tips of spruce boughs, removing as much stem as you can easily. Add it to another small pan of boiling water. Remove from the heat and let it steep for 15 minutes. Again strain the mixture through the sieve into the gallon container, discarding the spruce tips.

Now, for your first decision: honey versus molasses. Mix 1 pound of molasses or ½ pound of honey into a small pan of boiling water and put it into the gallon container. The next decision is whether or not to use lime. A 6-ounce jar of Rose's lime juice added to the gallon container is about right. Rose's is another grand tradition on British vessels. But, tradition aside, fresh lime squeezings are even better. Last, fill your gallon container nearly to the top with boiling water.

Now dump the hot water out of the Grolsch bottles and refill them with hot brew and snap the caps. After the filled bottles cool to room temperature, add ½ teaspoon of yeast mixture to each bottle. Let the tops just sit loosely on the bottles for several days before clamping them down tight. (If you snap the caps tight right away, the bottles tend to explode. It's no fun opening bottles dressed in your bomb-squad outfit.)

Let them set for another few days, chill, carefully release the pressure, decant, and drink. If you object to sediment in the bottles, let the mixture ferment in the gallon container for several days. Then carefully decant it into the Grolsch bottles, snap tight right away, and wait another few days.

Spruce beer contains about as much alcohol as any stout ale, but it's the vitamin C content that's important. In order to combat "that dreadful distemper the Scurvy," at least three bottles of the basic version daily meets the minimum requirement. A 500 mg tablet of vitamin C is better substituted by 26 bottles of our grog. Overdo it—drink to your health. And toast to Captain Cook.

...thanks would be
given to salmon
and venison
instead of turkey.

CHAPTER 24
VENISON: THANKSGIVING, SOUTHEAST ALASKA-STYLE

Suppose the Pilgrims had landed in Alaska rather than Plymouth Rock? We'd be having a different fare on our Thanksgiving table. I doubt if we'd be carving up a roast eagle, but we'd be feasting on the bounty of a rich land.

First of all, thanks would be given to salmon and venison instead of turkey. The salmon would have been wrapped in skunk cabbage leaves and baked in a fire pit on a rocky beach. Venison would have been skewered on sticks facing an open fire. Today, methods have changed. Aluminum foil has replaced skunk cabbage leaves. Barbecue pits have replaced open fires. Keeping close to the spirit of Thanksgiving, the feasts of Southeast Alaska Pilgrims might have evolved into some of the following recipes.

Baked Stuffed Salmon

Fresh skunk cabbage leaves can only be found in greenhouses at this time of year, so I recommend aluminum foil for baking. Head, fins, tail, and skin may be left on, but I usually peel the skin off just before serving. Rub light olive oil all over the fish before laying it in a foil-lined roasting pan. As options, place thickly sliced onions, potatoes, celery, and carrots beneath the salmon. Add a glug or two of dry white wine before sealing the foil. The vegetables prevent the bottom of the fish from overcooking, and the wine embellishes the process by steaming.

Stuff the fish, using clam stuffing from the next recipe. Excess stuffing can be placed inside the foil. Cover the stuffed fish with more foil. Bake at 450°F. Remember, for each inch of thickness at the salmon's thickest spot, cook for 10 minutes. Do not turn the fish during cooking.

After baking, you can use the liquids from the pan to make a velouté sauce. Heat 1 ounce of olive oil in a saucepan. Stir in 1 ounce of fine white flour. Let it bubble at bit, but don't let it brown. Slowly add, stirring all the while, a cup of pan liquids. Thin it out with milk, still stirring. The tastes of salmon, vegetables, and wine will cohabitate in memorable fashion.

Shoreline Stuffing

This shellfish stuffing complements fish with other flavors of the sea. Oysters can be substituted or added to the clams. Use freshly shucked clams and oysters if possible. The stuffing captures the flavor of the fresh juices.

For each cup of chopped clams, add 1 cup of cooked rice and 2 cups of stale bread crumbs. Mix in a jigger of rice vinegar. Add a handful of freshly chopped dill or half-a-handful of dried dill. If it looks dry, add clam broth or white wine or both.

Some stuffing special hints:

- An ounce of chopped bullwhip kelp pickles will add zest to the stuffing.

- For a healthy salt substitute in fish dishes, crush up some dried seaweed—it adds iodine and more minerals and the essence of the sea.

- To stuff the salmon, clean it well, then dry both insides and outsides with paper towels. For each pound of fish, you'll need about a cup of dressing. Pack the cavity with dressing by hand.

Roast Venison

The problem with venison roasts is that they're too lean and they tend to dry out during cooking. Some people drape strips of bacon on top of venison to add fat slowly throughout cooking. Others baste frequently during cooking. I suggest using a Dutch oven or a roasting pan with a lid. Add some hearty burgundy or red zinfandel wine to keep the venison from drying out. Cook at 300°F until tender.

Serve the roast with your choice of relishes, stuffing, and sauces. I've listed one of each, all based upon cranberries, naturally abundant in Alaska.

Cranberry Ketchup

This recipe calls for highbush cranberries. For lowbush or store-bought cranberries, I'd use less sweetening. I usually specify honey instead of sugar, but in this case, brown sugar works well. Cranberry Ketchup can be used like any tomato ketchup, but the highbush version sparkles when used with venison and other game. The wild and gamy highbush cranberry differs in taste from the lowbush cranberry, and their ketchups will differ as well.

Boil 4 cups of cranberries with 1 chopped onion. When the berries and onion are almost soft, pulverize them with a sieve or food processor. For highbush cranberries, use the sieve or strain to remove the large seeds. Place them in a pot, and add 2 cups of brown sugar (or 1 cup of honey) and 1 cup of white vinegar. Simmer until thickened. Now add powdered spices—cinnamon, allspice, cloves—to your taste, starting with 1 teaspoon each. This ketchup keeps well in the refrigerator, but it can also be put up in jars and preserved by boiling-water canning.

Afterthoughts on cranberries: add mashed rose hips to cranberry recipes. Less cooking is better for dishes rich in vitamin C, such as those with rose hips and cranberries. Add spices at the end of the cooking process, since heat only destroys their potency.

Cranberry Stuffing

Chop up ½ onion, a stalk of celery, including leaves, and a handful of parsley. Sauté them in light olive oil until barely soft. Grind or finely chop 2 cups of cranberries. For highbush cranberries, boil them first for a minute or two, then strain them to remove the seeds. Add 1 cup of brown sugar. Mix all of this into 6 cups of stale bread crumbs. If it seems too dry, add white wine.

Cranberry Sauce for Venison

When the roast venison is done or nearly done, add cranberry relish to the juices from the roasting pan. Cranberry relish follows the same procedure as Cranberry Ketchup, described above, except that the relish version omits vinegar and spices. The sauce can be fortified with a splash of burgundy wine. If you have cranberry wine or cranberry liquor, those might make a good sauce addition as well.

So, Pilgrims, spare the roast turkey, spare the roast eagle. Instead, pay your respects to the salmon and deer of Alaska. They honor us with their sacrifice and, for that, we can give thanks.

"Then let them
eat bait."

Chapter 25

Daring Fare:
Bombers, Bait,
and Whistlepigs

"**Y**our highness, the people have no salmon."

"Let them eat bombers."

"But your highness, the people have no bombers."

"Then let them eat bait."

The universe always runs downhill. Someday, perhaps soon, we'll drink beer and reminisce about the good old days when we shook off those ugly bombers, as Irish Lords are known in Alaska, clubbed them into unconsciousness to teach them not to hook themselves on our gear, and watched eagles swoop down and snatch them out of our wake. Not me—I keep bombers; they taste great. In fact, I've got an Irish Lord recipe that's outstanding. Just put a sack over their heads and treat them like fish.

Someday perhaps we'll realize the economy of harvesting the lower links of the food chain and discover, as the more sophisticated seafood eating cultures have long ago discovered, that what we Alaskans consider "bait" usually tastes better than what we're fishing for. The sooner we set aside our artificial, ridiculous notions about herring, squid, octopus, and the like, the better. And to prove my points, I challenge you with the following recipes.

Bomber/Bait Bouillabaisse

In the beginning, bouillabaisse had a simple, humble Mediterranean origin as an inexpensive, working fisherman's fish stew. It contained fish from the catch of the day and, undoubtedly, leftover bait. It should contain as many types of fish as there are available. The ideal bouillabaisse would contain all the fish of the sea. The only rule is that they must be fresh. Restaurateurs shanghaied the recipe, threw in expensive ingredients (not at all what the local fishermen had in mind—most controversially, lobster and crab), charged outrageous prices, and constantly bickered among themselves about degrees of authenticity. The following recipe reverts back to the original theme.

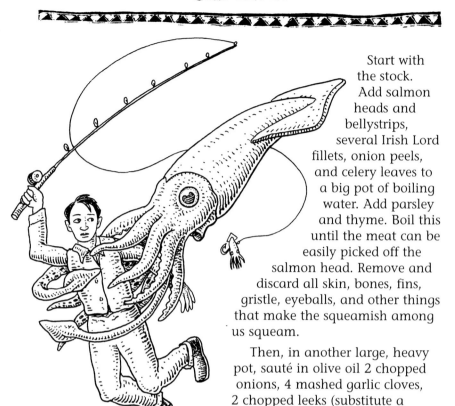

Start with the stock. Add salmon heads and bellystrips, several Irish Lord fillets, onion peels, and celery leaves to a big pot of boiling water. Add parsley and thyme. Boil this until the meat can be easily picked off the salmon head. Remove and discard all skin, bones, fins, gristle, eyeballs, and other things that make the squeamish among us squeam.

Then, in another large, heavy pot, sauté in olive oil 2 chopped onions, 4 mashed garlic cloves, 2 chopped leeks (substitute a bunch of green onions for a leek), and 4 stalks of celery, chopped. Add spices: fennel seed, pepper, more thyme, basil, bay leaves, chives, bell pepper, celery seed, rosemary, and especially, saffron. Saffron is essential to bouillabaisse. If you don't add saffron, you can have an excellent fish chowder, but you can't have bouillabaisse.

Once the onions begin to turn transparent, add 2 cans of Italian-style pear tomatoes, 1 pint of clam juice, and a bottle of chablis. Add some of the stock prepared earlier. Whatever stock is left over should be frozen—it performs wonders as a poaching liquid to revitalize stale or too-long frozen seafood.

As soon as this mixture begins boiling, add the weird seafood. Throw in fillets of Irish Lord, cod, herring, and whatever Uglies are normally discarded. Then add clams, best with shells intact. Return to boiling and simmer for 10 minutes, no longer. Just before the time is up, mix in chopped or ringed squid mantles. Remove from the heat and serve with garlic French bread and another bottle of chablis. Now you're eating the authentic bouillabaisse, free of frills, an adventure into the future of exquisite cuisine, almost free of charge. Also serve with bowls of aioli and rouille (you can find the recipes in earlier chapters) and crouton rounds made from baguettes. Spread the aioli or rouille onto the rounds and float them in the bouillabaisse. Bouillabaisse is also served over potato slices boiled in a saffron broth.

IT'S A THIN LINE

BETWEEN LOVE AND BAIT

Author's Disclaimer: Do not eat bait, as in herring packaged as bait. It's low quality. You may as well eat canned cat food. Buy or catch only the fresh, human-quality herring, squid, etc. There's a rumor that bait processors still impregnate their products with saltpeter, which would make eaters thereof impotent, supposedly a legacy from a Nazi conspiracy to eliminate inferior genes from impure stocks of mongrelized fishermen. This is untrue, except for the message: don't eat bait-quality herring. I've tried it. It's nasty, even with the designer sauces.

Squid Salad

I almost hate to write about this. It's getting to be a fad. Faddists call squid "calamari." This causes prices to skyrocket. The word is out. Squid tastes similar to but is better than abalone. Sadly, it is almost always cooked improperly—as is abalone. Follow this method to see what the gods meant squid to taste like. Have a huge pot of water boiling rapidly, very rapidly. Add chopped squid, whether mantles, rings, or tentacles (I prefer to save my tentacles for tempura). There should be so much water that boiling should not stop upon the addition of the squid.

Boil for 30 seconds. Not 35, but 30. Immediately remove the squid and run them under cold water. That is all. Marinate the cooked squid in a chilled olive-oil vinaigrette for several hours. Serve with your choices of red bell peppers, marinated artichoke hearts, bean sprouts, green onions, avocado, mushrooms, spinach, and, if you must, lettuce.

There are thousands of ways to cook squid. Almost every culture except, of course, ours has fantastic squid recipes. This is a delectable way to begin what should be a beautiful relationship with one of the finer weird creatures of the sea. They probably say the same of us. Who is to know?

Bombers and bait of today are the food of royalty of tomorrow. As salmon stocks decline and now undisturbed Irish Lord stocks improve their gene pool, who knows whereof the evolutions of fish and the human appreciations thereof shall lead. You can be on the leading edge by eating weird.

Watch out!

You Want Fries with That?

When you've run out of bombers and bait, your next option for survival is cooking those land animals that most people would not consider. This is your reality TV recipe.

Joel's Mongol Marmot

When in Mongolia, you do as the Mongolians do. Joel came back with a popular marmot treatment. This is also your rolling-blackout contingency recipe.

To cook Joel's Mongol Marmot, start by building a fire around the right-sized rocks. To find the right sizes, slit open the marmot and clean out the guts. The rocks are sized to fit in the abdominal cavity. Find nice, round ones. Once the rocks are up to fire-temperature, point your marmot nose-down and fill her up. Then sew up the abdominal cavity. Use a propane torch (yes, all modern Mongols carry them) to burn off the hair and scorch the skin charcoal-like, crispy like our roast pig on the spit. Give your hot rocks enough time to bake from the inside.

I can't divulge the details on the traditional Mongol Marmot presentation. They're outside our Envelope of Social Decency. You'll have to carve it up according to your own abilities.

In Mongolia, some marmots carry the plague, but our whistlepigs in Alaska are USDA-certified plague-free. The delicate aroma of whistlepig roasting outdoors is as much a sign of spring as Groundhog Day. Enjoy.

...whistlepigs in Alaska
are USDA-certified
plague-free.

FISHIN': IMPOSSIBLE

"Your fishin, should you decide to accept it, is to land the lunker of your life despite harrowing odds. Your line is horribly tangled, your buddy's been consumed by a crazed brown bear, insects are eating you alive, you're two days overdue at the office, I.R.S. agents are stalking you and your spouse is sick of your fish obsession. Good luck. You'll need it pal. This reel will self destruct in ten seconds."

SECTION 4
THE ALASKA SMELTING POT

   As you travel through Alaska, you appreciate
our variety of cultures and cuisines. Coastal Alaska
first saw the Aleut and Tlingit and Haida,
who thrived on the seafood and intertidal life.
The Russian fur traders then settled on the Coast,
centered first in Kodiak and then in Sitka.
The Hudson's Bay Trading Company flag flew
briefly near Juneau, but thankfully the British
so-called cuisine has not lingered. Norwegians
settled in Petersburg, and the Little Norway
Festival, celebrating their independence day,
is a seafood feast in mid-May. Filipino and Chinese
cuisines followed influxes of cannery workers.
The Japanese buy much of our seafood now, and
their tastes for seafood have influenced our lives.
Our oil workers tend to enjoy Cajun food.
We Alaskans all enjoy catching what we eat
and cooking it according to what we were
brought up with.

The most
encountered Russian
fish recipe...
is piroghi.

CHAPTER 26
A TASTE OF RUSSIAN AMERICA

With all the Russian Orthodox churches around Alaska, you'd figure there'd be a heritage of Russian cooking. The most encountered Russian fish recipe that stands out consistently in the various community cookbooks is piroghi: a rice, cabbage, and fish pie also called *pirok, pirog,* or *peroche.* Don't confuse piroghi with *pirozhki,* a small pie, eaten out of the hand.

Piroghi—With Salmon

Most of the Piroghi recipes begin with dough that is rolled out into a baking dish. I'm not into this kind of punishment, so use store-bought frozen pie pastry plates. Nevertheless, you'll need a small amount of dough to cover the top of the pie. Using a fork, mash and mix an ounce of shortening or margarine into a cup of flour, and stir in one or two jiggers of water. This will make enough dough to cover two Piroghi pies.

Cover the bottom of the pie plate with a layer of cooked rice. Then add a layer of fish chunks or strips. On top of the fish, spread out a layer of sautéed shredded cabbage and chopped onion. On top of the cabbage-onion, spread out another layer of cooked rice. Cover with the top crust of rolled-out dough and cut some slits in the crust to let out steam. Bake at 350°F for 1 hour if the fish is uncooked, ½ hour if the fish is cooked.

One Sitka-based recipe specifies white king salmon as the fish of choice for Piroghi. A white sauce made from white king salmon poaching liquid with nutmeg and chives and added to the Piroghi sounds overwhelming. Other recipes call for halibut and omit the cabbage. Another source suggests the dried spinal nerve of sturgeon for Piroghi. Salmon works well; sockeye is my favorite.

Those who forage for the summer *pirok* could add wild celery (known by its Russian name *po'ochki*), beach lovage (*petru'shki*), or goosetongue (especially teamed up with potatoes), silverweed root, or various beach greens. As before, all chopped and mostly precooked. Serve slices of Piroghi hot or freeze it for later.

Christmas Dinner in the New World

When Christmas caroling in Russian America, be prepared to drink black tea laced with essences of cloves and rum and to eat hearty hot slices of *pirok*. *Pirok*, a traditional Slavic yuletide treat, has followed fur hunters into Alaska where it's still popular with Russian descendants and anybody else with good taste.

When cooked as finger-sized tarts, *pirok* becomes the diminutive *pirozhki*, little pies. Whether big or little, these pies can be easily frozen and reheated. *Pirozhki* can be made by rolling out the dough and cutting it into thin 4-inch circles. Place a dollop of the *pirok* filling in the center, fold up the edges, flip it over, and bake it until done. Say at 400°F degrees for a half hour or less. Serve with a cheese sauce and a Christmas carol.

Borscht with Fish

Most borscht recipes list ham or sausage as options. Smoked salmon can (and should) be substituted for ham in most recipes. Smoked salmon, also, works well with borscht. Trim and peel a couple of beets, parsnips, carrots, and potatoes, cut them into thin slices, and then cut the slices into matchstick-sized slivers. Chop an onion and a couple of celery stalks. Shred ½ head of cabbage. Add all the above to a quart of vegetable stock, made from the strained trimmings and peelings of all the above vegetables. Add a generous splash of vinegar, 1 cup of tomato juice, and boil all this for a half hour. Just before serving, add some chunks of smoked salmon and a dollop of sour cream. Garnish with croutons, parsley, and dill.

Braised Sturgeon with Garlic Flambé

A good 2 or 3 days before the meal, prepare the flambé sauce: grind or puree a whole bulb of garlic, or at least 10 cloves of garlic; spoon the garlic goo into a jar and add twice that volume of vodka; cover and refrigerate. About a day before, marinate the sturgeon steaks in some of the garlic-vodka sauce. Place the fish and marinade in Ziploc bags to spare the rest of your refrigerator contents. Broil the sturgeon steaks on the barbecue grill and place on a flameproof plate.

At serving, heat up a metal ladle, decant some garlic-flavored vodka into the ladle, carefully ignite the contents, and pour the flaming vodka over the sturgeon steaks. Out of sturgeon? Try sablefish.

Botvinyua—A Cold Salmon Soup

Poach about 2 pounds of salmon, chill, and cut into chunks. Clean carefully, trim, and puree a pound of fresh spinach leaves. Do likewise with ½ pound of sorrel. If you can't get sorrel (which grows wild as sourdock), substitute more spinach and the juice of a lemon. In a large serving bowl, mix the spinach and sourdock together and add a glug or two of dry white wine and the juice of 1 lemon. Peel a cucumber and cut it into strips. Chop a bunch of green onions into 2-inch lengths. Add the chilled salmon chunks, cukes, and onions to the spinach-sorrel puree. Garnish with sprigs of dill and place dishes of sour cream and horseradish nearby.

Various Russian Fish Appetizers

Don't forget caviar. Try cured salmon eggs, sometimes sold as ikura, with cream cheese on dark rye bread, with green onions on the side. A fake caviar can be made with a cup of chopped black olives, an ounce of mashed anchovies, and a dash of pureed garlic. On pickled or kippered herring, use Russian mustard sauce: mustard with mayonnaise, capers, and chopped green onion. Add chopped beets, onions, and boiled potatoes to pickled or kippered herring for a Russian salad.

With the exception of the braised sturgeon, most of these recipes can be whipped up easily and quickly, which, if you've got a Russian patrol boat astern, will be a convenience, *da?*

SOMETIMES LATE AT NIGHT THE SPIRITS OF ALL THE FISH
I'VE EVER CAUGHT COME BACK TO HAUNT ME.

My scrawled Notes
betray my
hedonism.

CHAPTER 27
VIKING VITTLES

"Never plunder on an empty stomach."
—Lars the Awful, 879–917 A.D.

The original power-lunchers poached their fish on inverted chest armor. Often at midday, hungry Vikings would pause to enjoy a seafood lunch that would provide health, stamina, and virility and give the opportunity to profit from a more effective pillage lunch strategy.

One May, I sailed to Petersburg, Alaska, for the Little Norway Festival so that I could collect some authentic Scandinavian seafood recipes from the Vikings and Valkyries plundering about in local drinking and eating establishments. The seafood layouts at the Little Norway Festival have to be eaten to be believed. Although strictly dedicated to culinary research, I was forced to drink and eat copiously in order to keep from blowing my cover. My scrawled notes betray my hedonism.

If *pirok* has followed the Russians, lutefisk has followed those who came to Alaska from Norway. The Christmas meal in Petersburg will feature this cured cod with boiled potatoes and mashed rutabagas. Lutefisk has become legend. The hushed mention of the word will awaken a dead audience, evoke rude comments, stimulate questionable ethnic jokes, and create generic uproar. Some think it inedible. I like the idea of fish for Christmas, so I'm giving it another try. This year, I think I have the formula.

Lutefisk

Lutefisk is cured in a caustic lye solution and then usually frozen. Methods of curing lutefisk by lye are as varied as methods of smoking fish. They say that curing lutefisk is like the legislative process—it's not something you want to see in the making.

The first steps in the lutefisk cooking process are those intended to revive it and undo the curing. Frozen lutefisk should be thawed slowly for several days in the refrigerator. It should then be soaked for 2 to 24 hours. Some sources say to use the juice of a lemon in 2 quarts of water. Others say to use milk. Others say salt water, the saltier water makes firmer final products. Rinse the lutefisk well prior to cooking.

Cooking lutefisk is simple. You can boil it or bake it. Boil it in seawater, salt water, or milk about 10 minutes for each inch of thickness. Bake it tightly wrapped in foil at 375°F. For baking options, rub the lutefisk with peppercorns and add a couple of dabs of butter. Poke a hole in the foil and drain off the fluids. You might save the fluids for a sauce. And then, you might not.

For side dishes, have boiled potatoes and mashed turnip or rutabaga. Keep it simple.

Traditionally, lutefisk is served with melted butter or a white sauce, perhaps made with the milk used in poaching. This year, my twist in the formula will be a flambé with anisette. When ready to eat, have the lutefisk on the table and guests well clear of the danger area. Preheat an empty long-handled saucepan over the stove. Remove the pan from any source of flame and carefully add several ounces of anisette to the pan. Be careful of boilover. From the side, using a match or lighter to the lip of the pan, ignite the anisette and pour the blue flaming liqueur over the lutefisk on each plate. Don't mess it up by burning the tablecloth. Fire extinguisher foam and lutefisk don't mix.

Or do they?

Mead

Start with homemade mead, an easily made grog. Add ½ pound of honey to 3 quarts of boiling water. Pour this mixture into the fermenting vessel. Cool to room temperature and add some lukewarm yeast-sugar solution. Ferment for 3 to 10 days, decant carefully, and drink from tankards.

Salmon and Spinach Soup

Another good beginning is Salmon and Spinach Soup. Boil some salmon belly-strips, tails, heads, bones, or whatever is at hand. Pick the meat and throw away the waste. Now add fresh spinach, watercress, and green onions and return to boiling for a minute or so. Once cooled, blend until uniformly mixed. Refrigerate. Upon serving add chunks of cucumber and sour cream. Spice with dill.

Gravlax

Gravlax is a wonderful lox-style Scandinavian salmon delicacy. Start with boneless fillets, skins intact. For each pound of fillet, mix up 1 ounce of salt, ½ ounce of honey, 2 ounces of brandy, several sprigs of dill, and ground white pepper to taste. Massage the mixture into the salmon. With skin side up, place a plate on the salmon. Weight the plate down with 2 pounds of something. Refrigerate for 24 hours. Flip the salmon and refrigerate for another 24 hours. Repeat.

Slice the fillets thinly, very thinly, on a steep diagonal, at least 45 degrees. To preserve for up to a week or more, place the sliced gravlax in a jar and add olive oil. Keep cool. Serve on the darkest pumpernickel available, with sweet mustard sauce. For each ounce of mustard (dijon), add ½ tablespoon of honey, 2 tablespoons of wine vinegar, and 1 teaspoon of fresh chopped dill. Slowly add ⅓ cup of olive oil, beating constantly with a fork.

Salmon Tartare

For serious plunderers, salmon tartare is in order. Grind coarsely (or chop finely) the freshest skinless salmon fillet available. Add the juice of a lemon, chopped shallots (substitute white parts of green onions), capers, ground white pepper, dill weed, and a beaten raw egg. Mix thoroughly and chill. Serve on rye bread.

Boiled Fish

For breakfast, boil fish and quartered potatoes about 10 minutes. Top it off with a poached or soft-boiled egg. Serve with hollandaise or English sauce, depending upon your mood. Hollandaise sauce can be a nuisance, and if you're willing to sacrifice, you can substitute by mixing mustard with mayonnaise and adding a dash of pepper. English sauce: sauté mushrooms in butter, add flour and thicken with cream; add pepper.

Curried Seafood Sandwich

Seafood sandwiches aren't common enough. This one packs shrimp and asparagus spears between Swedish rye with a curry sauce. Curry sauce: mix 1 teaspoon of curry powder with ¼ cup of mayonnaise.

Fish Cakes

Eastonsen's fish (or crab) cakes are to be tried. Add equal amounts of cooked fish (or crab) and crumbled stale white bread (less crusts). A raw egg glues it together, about 1 egg per 2 servings. Add milk to get it to a gooey consistency so that it can be worked into balls. Spice it with ginger and chopped green onions. Fry the balls in ½ inch of oil.

Troll's Fish Cakes

Our flaky cookbook artist has his ideas on how to cook, even though I don't tell him how to art. Ray claims this recipe came from Petersburg. It's his New Year's feast to clean out the freezer from the previous year's catch.

Ingredients:

2 cups boiled and flaked potatoes, Yukon Golds
1 cup cooked salmon, in small flakes
1 cup cooked halibut, cod, or rockfish, in small flakes
½ cup onion, chopped in small pieces
2 eggs, lightly scrambled
1 teaspoon nutmeg (the "secret" ingredient)
1 teaspoon allspice
White pepper to taste
Dill to taste
Basil to taste

Mix up these ingredients, form into patties, and fry in peanut oil. Serve with grated cheddar cheese.

Fish Baked in Rye Bread

For dinner, bake fish and potatoes in rye bread. Slice the cap off a large loaf of dark rye or pumpernickel bread. Scoop out most of the insides. Add chunks of fish and sliced potatoes, filling the cavity. Spice with dill. Replace the cap and bake at 350°F until cooked, about 30 minutes.

Salmon Flambé

Another dinner treat is Salmon Flambé. Broil or barbecue salmon fillets in butter and tarragon. Place in a flameproof dish. At serving time, add a saucepan of heated Pernod (or any other anise-flavored liqueur) that has been ignited. Serve with side dishes of chopped green onions and other garnish.

Scandinavian Weed

Dill is the mainstay of Scandinavian spices. Both the leaves and seeds are used in cooking. Dill is a great houseplant, and its weed-like tenacity makes it hard to kill. As with most herbs, freshly picked dill has little resemblance to what is sold in jars. Dill has remarkable attributes. It reduces swelling, eases pain, increases milk for nursing mothers, and relieves flatulence. What more could you ask for? Add some sprigs to a jar of vinegar. Mix it with sour cream for a simple yet excellent sauce. Great stuff, dill, and it's destined to make seafood attain greatness. Use it often.

Heather's Horseradish Sauce

Heather's Horseradish Sauce goes with any Scandinavian seafood. In 8 ounces of sour cream (or half sour cream and half plain yogurt), add the juice of a lemon, a chopped clove of garlic, dill seed, dill weed, and lots of horseradish—at least 1 ounce.

Well-fixed seafood inspires plunderers to new heights of performance. It's healthy and promotes long life. Lars the Awful wouldn't lead you wrong.

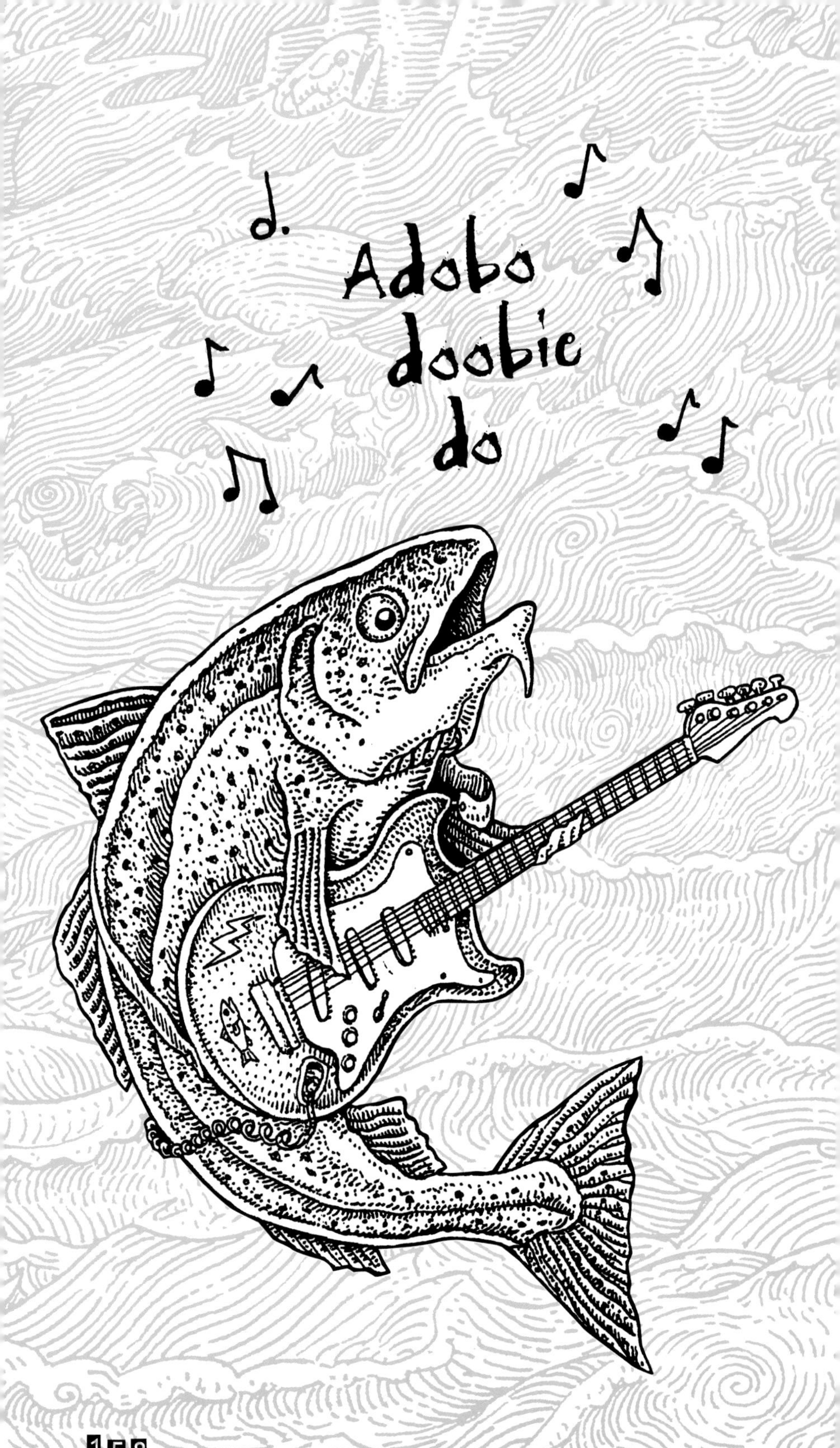
Adobo
doobie
do

Chapter 28

Filipino:
Secret Cuisines
of Alaska

The Philippines cradled the melting pot of several cultural cuisines, mixing the imperial Spanish influence with that of the Chinese and the Pacific Islanders. We in Alaska find ourselves enriched with the flavors of the Filipino community: vinegar and soy sauce, garlic, and ginger.

Adobo stands as the mainstay of Filipino cuisine in Alaska. The local cookbooks and Filipino restaurant menus feature chicken, pork, venison, and seafood versions of Adobo. Several styles of Adobo can be found in various references, so I've included four examples. Some recipes take several minutes to cook, and others take several hours.

Angoon-Style Adobo

I mention Angoon, Alaska, because of their *The Great Angoon Cookbook*, which I recommend for its insights to the natural foods of Southeast Alaska, the cultural methods of cooking, and the heritage of the people of Angoon. Between the recipes for "Octopus Burgers" and "Halibut Quiche," you'll find out about "Trapping a Bear in the Old Days" and "How to Snare a Deer."

The cookbook begins with several superior Angoon versions of Adobo, and with instructions such as "Put all ingredients in a pot. Cook until done." Adobo recipes call for chicken, pork, and venison. Here's my favorite, slightly modified because of my addictions to garlic and ginger.

Cut up a chicken into bite-sized pieces. Place these in a large skillet and add 4 ounces of cider vinegar and 2 ounces of soy sauce. Add some water or red wine and begin to simmer. Add 1 chopped onion, 4 to 10 minced garlic cloves, and 1 or 2 inches of ginger root, grated. Place 2 ounces of pickling spices in an infuser or wrap them in cheesecloth. Simmer for 1 hour. Serve with white rice.

You may want to make a sauce from the skillet juices. Strain the juices to remove the chunky parts. For each cup of sauce, dissolve 1 tablespoon of cornstarch into a small amount of cold water.

Slowly stir the cornstarch into the simmering skillet juices until it looks right.

If you can't find pickling spices at the store, you can mix some up. For this recipe, I'd use coriander seeds, cloves, mustard seeds, allspice, bay leaves, turmeric, and mace. Other ingredients can include cinnamon, red pepper, black pepper, caraway, dill seed, and fennel. Have fun.

With these spices, vinegar, and soy, imagine Adobo venison put up in the canning method. The pressure cooker would tenderize even the toughest venison, and the pickling spices would have months to infuse into the meat.

Crispy-Style Fried Adobo

This version follows the Angoon style, with a sequel. Make the Adobo as above and remove it from the skillet after it's almost well done. Remove and dry the chunks of chicken, pork, or whatever on paper towels. Then, using a cast-iron skillet on high heat, fry the Adobo meat chunks in cooking oil until they're browned and crispy on the outside. Serve with white rice, steamed vegetables, and sauce. You might try the skillet sauce as above or another tart sauce, like Cranberry Ketchup.

Fast-Food-Style Adobo

This style takes less than 15 minutes, from chopping block to table. Chop lean beef into bite-sized pieces. Smash and mince 10 cloves of garlic. In a lightly oiled, smoking-hot cast-iron skillet, sauté the garlic for 30 seconds. Add the beef and sear it at high heat for 6 minutes, stirring frequently. Open the windows and expect smoke to billow forth.

Meanwhile, with your other hand, mix together ½ cup of vinegar and ½ cup of soy sauce. Remove the beef from the skillet. Then, at arm's length, add the vinegar/soy mixture, which will foam and steam up the place. Stir the vinegar/soy mixture so as to scrape all the beef residue from the bottom of the skillet. When the liquid volume has been reduced by half, serve it over the beef over white rice.

Pusit Adobo

Squid also makes for fast-cooking adobo. If the sound of "squid" would make your eaters squeamish, tell them it's "calamari," the Italian name, or better, *pusit*, the Filipino name. Or since properly cooked squid tastes like abalone, tell them it's abalone.

You can buy two kinds of squid locally. Whole squid need to be cleaned. Chop off the tentacles and save them. Remove the insides and discard them. You can remove the skin if you want to, but it's tedious. Chop the body into rings, about ½ inch long. The second kind needs no cleaning and is sold as squid "steak." It's the mantle of a larger species and looks like a white pancake.

Begin with the garlic: smash and mince 10 or more cloves. Add them and 2 ounces of cooking oil to a heavy saucepan over high heat. Sauté the garlic for 2 minutes, then add about 3 cups of dry short-grained rice. Let the rice sauté for 2 more minutes.

Chop up about 2 pounds of squid and a large onion into bite-sized pieces. Mix these into the saucepan and sauté for another 2 minutes. Now add ½ cup of white vinegar and ½ cup of soy sauce. After 2 more minutes, add 4 cups of fish or chicken stock. Reduce the heat to a simmer and cover the pan. Do not stir during cooking. Peek every so often and add a little more water if it dries out. It's ready in 20 minutes or less. Garnish with tomato slices and parsley.

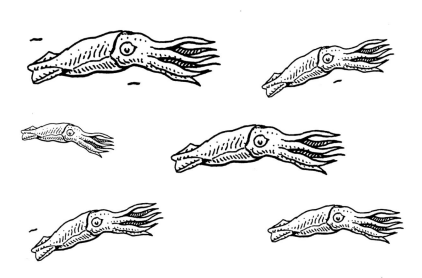

I'm weary of
greasy eggs and
synthetic hash brown
potatoes.

CHAPTER 29
INTERNATIONAL SEAFOOD BREAKFASTS

What this country needs is a good 5-cent breakfast. But if I couldn't get breakfast for a nickel, my second choice would be for a quality seafood breakfast; I'm weary of greasy eggs and synthetic hash brown potatoes. Other countries have good seafood breakfasts. Why can't we?

The thought of caviar and champagne, smoked salmon and bagels, and a scallop quiche sets my Sunday breakfast taste buds into a feeding frenzy. With that Gallic setting for a beginning, let's continue the theme with a breakfast tour of European seafood cuisine.

Ya Sure Fish Breakfast

Any Scandinavian worth his or her salt cod will eat fish to start the day. This is one of my favorites for an on-board breakfast. It's easy to make mass quantities for a large crew and can be cooked in one pot.

Ingredients for 1 very hungry person:

2 medium potatoes
2 eggs
4 ounces halibut or cod fillet
1 tablespoon melted butter
Pepper to taste
Chopped celery

Cut the potatoes into bite-sized pieces and place them in the bottom of a large pot of boiling water. Cut the fish fillet into 1-inch pieces and place them on top of the potatoes. When the boiling resumes, start your 10-minute clock. With 4 minutes to go on the clock, add the 2 eggs to the boiling water. When the time is up, drain the potatoes and fish, put them in serving dishes, and break the soft-boiled eggs over them. Add a tablespoon of melted butter, grind some pepper for spice and garnish with parsley. You betcha.

Fish Pasta Italiano

Here's a similar breakfast from the Mediterranean climes. Like the above recipe, this can be easily expanded to serve a multitude of breakfast diners. This is a single serving on the hearty side:

2 ounces olive oil, divided
1 teaspoon dried basil
2 eggs
2 ounces pasta, seashells or wide short noodles
1 ounce smoked salmon

In a large pot of boiling water, add half the olive oil and the dried basil. Cook the eggs until they're hard-boiled, usually about 10 minutes. After removing the eggs and peeling them, chop them into small pieces. Add the pasta to the still-boiling water and cook it until just barely done, usually less than 5 minutes, depending upon the type of pasta. Drain the pasta, add the rest of the oil and basil, and toss. Chop the smoked salmon into chunks, and mix it and the hard-boiled eggs into the pasta and serve quickly while it's still hot.

Seafood Quiche

Everyone has a favorite quiche recipe. Here's mine:

Ingredients for 4 servings:
1 tablespoon butter
4 ounces chopped shallots or the white parts of green onions
4 eggs
1 cup grated white cheese: Gruyère, Swiss, or the like
1 cup cream or half-and-half
6 ounces small, cooked shrimp
6 ounces chopped, cooked clams
1 9-inch piecrust

Using the butter, sauté the shallots until soft. Beat the eggs well and add all the ingredients. Pour into the piecrust and bake at 350 degrees for 30 minutes, until an inserted knife blade comes out clean.

Salmon Frittata

Italy's answer to quiche is easier because it does not involve a piecrust. You'll need your heaviest skillet, cast iron if you have it. Unlike omelets, frittatas are cooked slowly over very low heat, long enough to firmly set.

Ingredients for 4 servings:

1 tablespoon olive oil
1 small white onion, sliced thinly
2 zucchinis, sliced into thin disks
6 eggs
Pepper, freshly ground
6 ounces poached salmon, flaked
1 ounce butter
1 cup freshly grated Parmesan or Swiss cheese, divided
1 ounce parsley, chopped finely

Using the olive oil, sauté the onion and zucchini until the onion just turns transparent. In a large bowl, beat the eggs well and add a few twists of freshly ground pepper. Mix in the flaked salmon. Melt the butter in a large, heavy skillet until the butter bubbles but doesn't brown. Turn the heat down to low and add the egg-salmon mixture, the sautéed vegetables, and most of the cheese, reserving about an ounce of cheese for use later. Cook this slowly, until the eggs have set and only the top surface is runny; this may take a half hour. Add the remaining cheese and place the skillet under the broiler for a minute or so. Garnish with parsley.

Greece

Poached salmon, along with most everything else in Greece, would be served with the garlic sauce skordalia. Peel, quarter, and boil about 6 potatoes. In a food processor, puree about 6 garlic cloves. Once the potatoes are soft, add them piece by piece to the food processor containing the pureed garlic. While pureeing, add 2 egg yolks and slowly pour in ½ cup or more of olive oil. Now add 1 ounce of lemon juice and some black pepper. Adjust to taste by adding more oil or lemon juice. Pour over poached salmon.

Using dill and champagne and garlic, the Europeans have a delightful time when they can get their hands on some salmon. Practice up for your next trip abroad by trying it their way. *Bon appétit.*

CHAPTER 30
MEXICAN: CHILE PEPPERS, CHILE SALSA, AND CHILEHEADS

Native Americans have been eating chiles for over 9,000 years. When Columbus arrived in search of gold and spices, he thought he was in Asia. He called the Natives "Indians" and he called the chiles "peppers." He was wrong on both calls.

Chile peppers have become part of European and present-day American cuisine. When chile peppers or chile spices are cooked with meat, beans, or tomatoes, we call the dish "chili." Chileheads debate and argue, fume and fight over recipes and methods of authentic chile cookery.

The recipes and methods that I suggest will yield quick-cooking chiles, with crunchy onion flavors and mouth-expanding experiences. I'll begin with a zingy chile salsa that can punctuate several dishes other than chiles.

Chile Salsa

This multipurpose salsa plays several roles in chile fare. I add it both at the beginning and end of cooking chili and serve it as a table garnish for those who want an extra hit of chile excitement. I also use this Chile Salsa in other Mexican dishes, especially Ceviche, Snapper Veracruzano, and black beans. This salsa can last a week or three in the refrigerator before it ferments. Some folks prefer it fermented. Do not freeze it.

The Chile Salsa recipe calls for every variety of chile pepper you can lay your hands on, from the killer jalapeño to the gentler and kinder bell pepper. Use peppers that are yellow, green, and red, short, long, skinny, and fat. For those with adventurous tastes, I'd suggest 6 or more jalapeños, 1 yellow banana pepper, 1 California pepper, 1 green bell and 1 red bell pepper.

Be careful laying your hands on hot peppers, especially the jalapeños. They contain an incendiary oil that can blister your skin. Unless you enjoy pain and temporary blindness, do not rub your eyes after handling or chopping these peppers. Wear disposable kitchen gloves. Even if you wash your hands several times with soap, some eye-burning residue may remain on your skin for days.

Remove the stems, cores, and seeds from your selection of chile peppers and chop them finely. Chop and add a large bunch of cilantro. Also chop and add several cloves of garlic, several small plum tomatoes, a small red onion, and a bunch of green onions. If you're low on vitamin C, add chopped parsley. Squeeze in the juice of a lime and add a gurgle of olive oil.

Snapper Chili

Chili purists from Texas beef country would have cardiac arrest to hear of a chili recipe without beef and with fish, but that, after all, is the point. Once you try red snapper with red beans and red chile, you'll recover. This chili can use any firm white fish, such as rockfish (snapper), halibut, and swordfish.

In a large pot over medium heat, add a can of stewed tomatoes and a can of corn, both with juices. Add a can of kidney beans and a can of pinto beans, both without juices.

While this is heating up, chop a large yellow onion and sauté briefly in a skillet with some olive oil. Then chop up several tomatoes and add them to the skillet. Add a large handful of Chile Salsa to the skillet. After simmering for several minutes, dump all this into the large pot. You may need to add some water to cover the ingredients.

Cut the fish into inch-sized hunks. Add another handful of Chile Salsa to the fish chunks and let them marinate for several minutes. When the mixture in the large pot begins to simmer, carefully add the fish chunks and salsa and gently stir them into the mixture. After 10 minutes of simmering, the chili can be served. Place a large bowl of Chile Salsa on the table for those who wish to garnish.

Ahua Fish Chili

Another version is several alarms hot, so cut back on the obvious spices if you can't take it. Reconstitute, then cook ½ cup of dried red or kidney beans according to instructions (usually by boiling washed beans for a minute, letting them soak for an hour, and then boiling them for another half hour or so)—or just use a can of beans if you're in a hurry.

In a huge pot, sauté 2 chopped onions in olive oil, and add 2 chopped-up tomatoes, including seeds, 2 chopped jalapeño peppers, and 3 or 4 minced cloves of garlic. Once the onions are transparent, add spices: 2 tablespoons (!) of cayenne pepper powder, 3 tablespoons (!) of cumin, 1 tablespoon of dry mustard, 1 tablespoon of dried cilantro, and 1 tablespoon of paprika. Now add the drained beans, mix well, and flood the mixture with beer. Boil for 10 minutes and carefully add 1 pound of chunked red snapper. Boil for another 10 minutes and serve. Using precooked beans makes this preparation fast and easy. It is hot.

Sirloin Chili

This recipe follows the fish chili procedure with a few embellishments. Begin as before, with the large chili pot with beans, tomatoes, and corn and with the skillet with onions, tomatoes, and salsa.

Cut a pound of sirloin into bite-sized chunks. With a red-hot cast-iron skillet, sear the sirloin chunks for a minute or two, turning them often. Then turn down the heat to medium. As juices form, pour them off into the large chili pot. When the sirloin chunks are cooked, dump them into the chili pot, return the empty skillet to the fire, and turn up the heat.

As the skillet reheats, add 1 tablespoon of cumin seeds and toast them in the skillet. Now, add 1 cup of dry red wine to the skillet. Let the wine bubble and froth while you use a fork or spatula to scrape the meat residue from the bottom of the skillet. Then add the wine to the chili pot along with another handful of Chile Salsa. Serve right away.

Many chili recipes call for several hours of simmering. That's fine for tough cuts of beef. I'd add my onions, tomatoes, and Chile Salsa about 15 minutes before serving so that they'd still retain some flavor and nutrition.

Chocolate Chili

A subtle background hint of chocolate will surprise a good beef chili. Look for "mole" in the Mexican section of the market. Mix 2 ounces of mole in 1 cup of hot broth or hot water and add it batch-wise to a pot of chili, mixing and tasting as you go. If you can't find mole, try melting 1 ounce of unsweetened baking chocolate in 1 ounce of sesame oil.

Venison makes fine chili, as does pork, turkey, chorizo, and most anything you feel like. Try lentils instead of kidney or pinto beans. With chili, you can make things up as you go along. Chili makes great fuel for anarchists. Feel free to experiment and load up on the chiles.

Plunder from the Sea of Cortez

Our converted Newfoundland fishing schooner looks more like a pirate ship than a sailing charter boat. Perhaps it's both. The boat's name, the *Elias Mann*, rings of both. It's late afternoon in the southern Sea of Cortez. We're anchored off an island next to two Mexican shrimpers, coming to life just before the evening trawling runs. The captain and an attractive crewperson jump in the raft and roar over to the trawlers, armed with two cold six-packs of Carta Blanca. Our boarding party returns with four gallons of iced prawns, the best kind of loot.

They also scored three flatfish, five snapper, and some sun-dried manta ray. There's a grand Mexican style in cooking fresh seafood aboard a funky sailing vessel anchored in a Sea of Cortez sunset. I'll be passing along what I learned about cooking all this.

Flatfish Ceviche

The finely chopped flounder fillets made a fine Ceviche. Chop onion, tomatoes, parsley, and cilantro, and marinate everything in lime juice. It's ready to eat in an hour or so. This simple version was as good as any, but if you're into spice, add finely chopped jalapeño pepper.

Shrimp-Stuffed Avocado

The larders of the *Elias Mann* were filled with 10-cents-a-pound avocados. A few shrimp were boiled for salad duty. The avocados were halved. In mayonnaise, the peeled shrimp, some peas, and garbanzos were mixed, and the mixture was stuffed into the avocados.

Snapper Veracruzana

Another easy one. First, make a sauce. Chop an onion, a green bell pepper, and a tomato. Lightly sauté all this in olive oil. Lay out some snapper fillets in a baking dish and put the sauce on top. Bake at 350°F until done, probably 10 to 15 minutes. Go light on the hot spices for this one.

Snapper Frito

Take a small whole snapper, remove the scales, gills, and guts. Lay the snapper on its side. With a sharp knife, make 2 slashes in the flesh down to, but not through, the backbone or ribs. One slash should be from the forward edge of the top fin to just behind the gut cavity. The other slash should be parallel, but further aft. Repeat the process on the other side. The idea is to expose fish flesh for easy cooking. Next, the whole fish is dipped in melted butter, rolled in flour, and deep-fried.

Mojo de Ajo Sauce

A very popular sauce; goes well with a variety of grilled fish and prawns. Chop up a handful of garlic cloves. Sauté them over medium low heat in butter. When the chopped cloves blacken, the sauce is ready.

Manta Ray Tacos

The pretty, local crewperson, accomplice, and interpreter in the seafood raid told me the proper way to cook *mantaraya*. I explained that *mantaraya* was not common on the supermarket shelves of *Nord Americano*. She said *no problemo*, this recipe works well with sun-dried squid or beef jerky. I asked about moose jerky. Of this, she was not sure.

Begin by teasing the fibers apart and boiling them for 5 minutes or so to soften them up. Dry the fibers and sauté them in olive oil with chopped garlic, onion, and green bell peppers. Serve this rolled up in tortillas or as tacos.

Tequila Shrimp

This is my prize recipe booty from Mexico. Start by briefly sautéing shelled prawns in butter. Add a splash of white wine and another of orange juice. While this simmers away for a minute or two, heat up a metal ladle. Once it's hot, pour in a jigger of tequila and a splash of Pernod. Carefully but quickly touch a match to the side to ignite the ladle contents, and pour the flaming liquors onto the sautéing prawns. Total cooking time should be less than 10 minutes. Serve right away with cold Mexican beer.

If you use lobster in the above fashion, this becomes the house specialty at La Posada, a fine inn and restaurant next to the NAO Marina in La Paz harbor and the official retreat of our charter crew. Our ex-Alaskan captain earned his grubstake in the pirate-charter business by working in canneries, on the North Slope, and hand trolling. Several other charter sailing yachts and fishing boats, clean and sleek, stood at the modern NAO marina, tempting my checkbook.

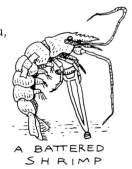

A BATTERED SHRIMP

You don't have to be aboard the *Elias Mann* to enjoy the seafood of the Sea of Cortez, but it sure helps.

Sampling Yucatecan-Style Cuisine

We secured our chain around a coral head, happily anchoring below the Mayan ruins of Tulum, on the eastern shores of Mexico's Yucatan peninsula. Soon our feet were being scorched on blinding white sand.

A few quick strides up the beach, at the lush jungle's edge, stood a rustic, palm-frond cantina, offering ice-cold Mexican beer. Orchids and seashells decorated the cantina walls. Lizards adorned the ceiling.

Behind the cantina, we found the owner tending a midday fire, over which lay a barracuda, split lengthwise and doubled back in halves held by a wire grill. The cantina owner, Rolando, basted the barracuda with a final dab of bright red sauce, then cut off a few chunks and invited us to a free lunch.

A gracious, delicious introduction to Yucatecan cuisine, that barracuda recipe was one of many collected on a recent trip to a blue-water paradise. The people of the Yucatan thrive on seafood: spiny lobster, shrimp, conch, octopus, snapper, and grouper. Toward the Peninsula's interior, the diet includes wild boar and venison, products of the jungle.

Achiote

The red spice in Rolando's barbecue sauce was Achiote, the mainstay of Yucatecan seasoning. To make Achiote paste, grind up annato seeds and stir in corn flour and vinegar. Make a sauce by mixing 1 ounce of paste with ½ cup of sour juice—vinegar, lemon juice, or juice from the local sour orange (or use equal amounts of orange and lemon juice). The locals use Achiote sauce to marinate and season all types of fish (not just barracuda) and meat, especially venison.

The Generic "Pibil"

The famous regional dish Cochinita Pibil is pork marinated in achiote sauce; covered with chopped tomatoes, onions, and hot peppers al gusto ("to taste"); wrapped in banana leaves; and steamed in an oven. If banana leaves are in short supply, aluminum foil can be used. Pibil-style recipes also include chicken and fish, and the results leave five-star memories. These dishes, listed as Pescado Empapelado on menus, owe their success to both the achiote marinade and the method of steaming, which retains the flavor while cooking the fish delicately.

Sopa de Lima

Seen on most Yucatecan menus, Lemon Soup normally contains shredded chicken. For seafood fans, shrimp can be substituted with equal success. For 4 servings, cut up 4 corn tortillas into quarters. Fry them in olive oil until very crisp and brown, and set them aside. Place 4 cups of water in a cauldron; add a sprig of mint, a handful of cilantro leaves, some oregano, black and red pepper, a clove, and a minced garlic clove. Bring all this to a boil.

Meanwhile, chop up a tomato and an onion; sauté in olive oil, and add them to the cauldron. Once boiling, throw in a pound or so of peeled shrimp. Return to a bare simmer, and then remove from the heat. Squeeze the juice from 2 lemons into the pot.

To serve, place the toasted tortillas in the bottom of large soup dishes; add soup, and garnish with thick slices of lemon.

Lobster Flambé

This meal was cooked at tableside over an alcohol burner. Preparation was accompanied by a guitarist singing a famous Mexican song about the love of a rooster for a dove, a tragic affair.

Melt a hunk of butter in a skillet. Toss in a few minced garlic cloves, add a lobster tail or two, shells removed, and sauté for a few moments. Add a dash of Worcestershire sauce and a dose of white wine. Simmer for a minute or two.

Remove from the heat and pour 2 jiggers of brandy into the skillet. When the brandy has warmed, swing the skillet over the burner to ignite it and, with a flourish, swirl the flaming contents about. Serve over white rice, alongside asparagus spears sautéed in butter, and with a glass of cold, dry white wine—to toast the rooster.

Sierra Ceviche

En route to Tulum, we caught a king mackerel, locally known as *sierra*. I thought of Ceviche before we landed it.

A poor loser, the *sierra* behaved badly once tossed aboard, snapping about and tearing up the place. We immobilized it by pouring tequila on its gills. I mean, within a microsecond after the tequila hit its gills, our *sierra* was incapable of anything more than a nearly undetectable quivering of its tail.

Generally, the longer you cook seafood, the worse it tastes. That's why Ceviche, equivalent to a mild pickling, rates as a favorite.

Ceviche, popular throughout Mexico and the Caribbean, is made with various fresh seafoods: conch, shrimp, octopus, shark, barracuda, bonito, grouper, tuna, squid, and any of the oily fish.

The Yucatecan treatment for Ceviche calls for local sour orange juice as marinade. Instead of sour orange, substitute equal amounts of lemon and orange juice, but also add an equal dose of lime juice. Chop up the fresh *sierra* fillets; cover with marinade, and add chopped onion, tomato, cilantro and hot pepper, al gusto. (Other recipes include oregano, parsley, green onion, cucumbers, tomato sauce, avocados, olive oil, mayonnaise, and all types of chiles.) In memory of the *sierra*, a splash of tequila is optional. Chill for a couple hours. Serve with tortilla chips that have been toasted by frying in olive oil.

When you visit Tulum, look up Rolando. He will put you in touch with a hammock, cold beer, and seafood caught by the local fishermen's cooperative. But don't wait for a trip to Tulum to try seafood cooked Yucatecan-style: barbecued over an open fire with achiote sauce, steamed while wrapped in banana leaves, or marinated as Ceviche.

Epilogue

After more beer and conversation, we found that owning the cantina was Rolando's sideline. It turns out that Roland has a Ph.D. in ecology, and his weekday job was managing the Yucatan state park system. He gave us inside tips on his favorite bird rookeries, undersea reefs, and orchid spots. We kept in touch and two years later, he and his family visited Juneau. They were as astonished with the mountains and the glaciers of Juneau as we were with the tropical fish and the ruins of the Mayans.

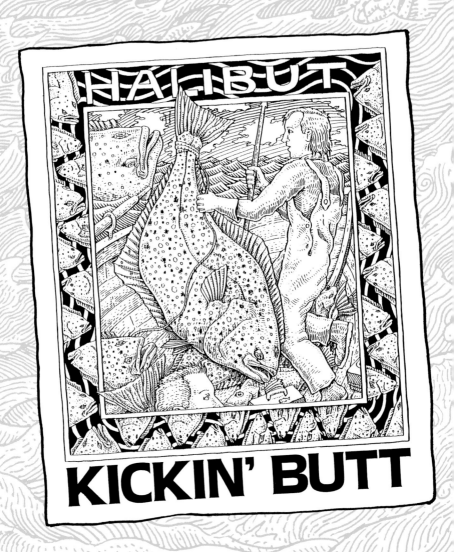

The secret is all-fresh ingredients.

CHAPTER 31
✦ CAJUN: GUMBO, ✦
ARMADILLO-STYLE

An interview with T. Terry Harvey, proprietor and cook at the Armadillo Restaurant near Juneau's downtown tour ship terminal, following a special dish of "Force 10 Filé Gumbo":

Q *Just how is it that a Tex-Mex restaurant can serve filé gumbo?*

A Well, certain of us Texans have been authorized by the State of Louisiana to make and sell filé gumbo. Besides, Louisiana gumbo and Texas chile share certain similar traits: they're both spicy and made from regional vegetables and other foods.

Q *And your gumbo is good?*

A Better than good. Queen Ida, during her last concert in Juneau, proclaimed our gumbo as the "best gumbo in the whole State of Alaska." She's performed here four times in the last five years and tasted our gumbo each time. She's writing a Cajun cookbook and says her gumbo recipe is very similar to ours.

Q *What's "filé"?*

A Ground-up sassafras leaves. We use it to thicken and spice the gumbo.

Q *So why doesn't your gumbo have any rice in it?*

A According to Queen Ida, there is no such thing as THE authentic gumbo recipe. There are thousands of variations. Each is as authentic as the other. Here again, gumbo is similar to chili.

Q *What ingredients do you use?*

A Seafood is the heart of our gumbo. In Louisiana, they use crab and shrimp. So here in Alaska, I choose Dungeness crab and Petersburg shrimp. The hard part is finding fresh okra. We have to use frozen okra sometimes.

Q *Let's talk about your salsa.*

A That's popular stuff. The crew from the Love Boat stops in each week to buy mass quantities of our salsa. I call it "two-alarm" salsa—spicy enough to deliver a mean zing, but not so hot that it overpowers you.

Q *And the secrets?*

A This is not like the wimpy salsa in supermarket jars. That's thoroughly cooked salsa with added preservatives.

Cooking takes the spice out of the spices. Our Armadillo Salsa is made fresh each week, which is about how long it lasts in the refrigerator. The secret is all-fresh ingredients: fresh cilantro especially, but also fresh tomatoes, fresh garlic, and fresh onions. But, you can't make our salsa if you don't have fresh cilantro.

Q *You use the salsa on seafood?*

A Sure. Sometimes we feature our Armadillo T. Terry's Snapper. At home, we use it to make Ceviche. Our salsa also goes into our barbecue sauces.

Q *Your barbecue sauce is used on seafood?*

A You betcha. When you're tired of salmon on the grill with the normal butter and brown sugar sauce, try our Armadillo Barbecue Sauce on snapper for variety. It has more of a zip. We use it for basting and cooking as well as dipping. It's like a sweet-and-sour sauce because it's got several flavors going all at once.

FARMED FISH

AREN'T THE ANSWER

Q *Well, what final Tex-Mex secrets can you pass along?*

A Spices are the key. Freshly ground black pepper, for example. Be generous with pepper. Add it at the last of the cooking cycle, too. Otherwise, the cooking tempers the flavor. Don't forget that great cayenne red pepper, either. Nope, you can't have enough pepper.

Now let's go into the specifics of the recipes.

Force 10 Filé Gumbo

Fry up 3 slices of bacon in a cast-iron skillet. Chop up 1 green pepper, 1 white onion, and 3 stalks of celery. Add these chopped vegetables to the skillet and sauté until lightly browned. In another large pot, boil 4 cups of chicken or fish stock, add 2 16-ounce cans of tomatoes and 1 8-ounce can of tomato sauce. Add the sautéed vegetables and 3 cups of chopped okra, fresh if you can find it, frozen if you can't. Simmer for 20 to 30 minutes.

Now make a roux. Using a hot cast-iron skillet, add 4 ounces of bacon grease and 2 ounces of flour. Stir constantly until the flour turns slightly brown. This may take up to 10 minutes. Then stir the roux in with the simmering vegetables.

Now add the seafood: the pickings from a good-sized Dungeness crab and a pound or so of Petersburg shrimp are the standard fare. (Of course, there are no rules in gumbo, so any seafood goes. So does chicken, ham, duck, oysters, and the like.) Cook the seafood for no more than 10 minutes. With a minute or two to go, add the spices: a tablespoon of filé powder, freshly ground coarse black pepper, red pepper, and any other peppers that suit your taste.

Serve with cornbread, French bread, or on rice. This recipe makes about 10 large bowls of filé gumbo.

Armadillo Salsa

Puree 10 fresh tomatoes in a blender, add a bunch of fresh cilantro, and a chopped white onion, and blend further so that the onion is in small chunks. In a small pan of boiling water, add ½ cup of dried red pepper flakes and simmer for 3 or 4 minutes until the pepper flakes are softened. Blend this into the tomato mixture. Add freshly minced garlic, cumin, and salt to taste.

Armadillo Barbecue Sauce

Slice up 2 lemons and boil them in a cup of water to which you've added 1 tablespoon of prepared mustard. After a few minutes of boiling, squeeze the juice from the lemons and discard the slices. Add 1 cup of white vinegar, 1 cup of Worcestershire sauce, 1 cup of tomato paste, ½ cup of Armadillo Salsa, and ½ cup of brown sugar. Let this simmer for 10 minutes or so, then add the spices: a tablespoon or 2 of freshly ground black pepper, minced garlic, and salt to taste. After adding the spices, remove the pan from the head. Use this sauce for barbecuing seafood, chicken, pork, and beef, and for serving on the table as an accompaniment.

T. Terry's Snapper

Sauté red snapper fillets in a cast-iron skillet with butter, lemon, and minced garlic. After 5 minutes, flip the fillets over. Sprinkle the cooked side of the fillet with sour cream, grated cheddar cheese, and a hefty layer of Armadillo Salsa. Cover the skillet and cook another 5 minutes. Don't overcook—the Golden Rule of Armadillo Fish Cooking. Finish with a crank on the handle of the pepper mill and guacamole as optional garnish.

Laurie's Cajun Spices

I like to make up a batch of this and keep it handy in the refrigerator in case I'm invaded by Cajuns. You can add this mixture to scrambled eggs, fried potatoes, or meatloaf. I prefer it with snapper or halibut as shown below.

Ingredients:

6 stalks celery, including leaves, chopped
2 mild green bell peppers, chopped
1 huge white onion, chopped
Olive oil
1 teaspoon black pepper
1 teaspoon white pepper
1 teaspoon mild red pepper
½ teaspoon dried thyme
½ teaspoon paprika
½ teaspoon powdered mustard
Salt to taste

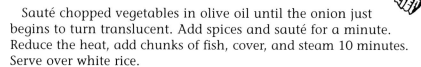

Sauté chopped vegetables in olive oil until the onion just begins to turn translucent. Add spices and sauté for a minute. Reduce the heat, add chunks of fish, cover, and steam 10 minutes. Serve over white rice.

CHAPTER 32

THAI: NOT FOR THE FAINTHEARTED

The well-known Thai beer bears the Sing-Ha label with the ornate image of a tiger. It takes a tiger of a beer to quench the dragon-hot spices of Thai food. Thai cooking blends East Indian with Chinese cooking styles and spices, sometimes curried and sometimes wokked. Hot and sour seafood recipes highlight shrimp, squid, and shellfish.

Before we discuss specific seafood recipes, let us examine the special ingredients that make Thai cuisine a hot item.

Resembling a green onion in looks, lemon grass resembles nothing in taste. For the only reasonable substitute, peel or grate the outer skin from a lemon. The peelings from one lemon skin equals one stalk of lemon grass—until you taste the difference, that is. The inner white parts of lemon grass can be eaten, but be sure to remove the green parts before serving; they're too tough to eat, but their flavor enhances the pot.

Fish sauce looks like soy sauce but tastes like anchovies. The best substitute is to crush a couple of salty anchovy fillets in a cup of water. Anchovy paste would do as well. Do not substitute soy sauce. Do not put your nose near a bottle of fish sauce. Just use it and have faith.

A hardy perennial weed, mint serves alongside Thai food as garnish. Thai food lifts mint to higher, almost holy, duty.

A bowl of cilantro leaves sits beside the bowl of mint leaves. Grab a handful and toss them into any seafood entree. This kind of addition makes cilantro, also known as Chinese parsley, the most popular herb worldwide.

Hot peppers. You bet they are—hotter than Mexico, hotter than Belize, hotter than Hell. These incendiary peppers bring beads of sweat to your forehead. No amount of milk, beer, arsenic, or liquid helium can relieve the pain. Tears evaporate on your cheeks. Your wisdom teeth will be retarded in growth. Be careful.

Also be careful when chopping Thai peppers in the kitchen. Never rub your eyes after chopping or handling peppers. Some say to rub your hands with salt or vinegar to remove the residue. Others suggest disposable rubber gloves. My favorite hands-off method is to puree hot peppers in a food processor or blender. A great Thai dipping sauce consists of hot pepper puree in a bowl of fish sauce. Dried chile peppers can be reconstituted by simmering and soaking in rice wine vinegar. You can also purchase Thai peppers as a paste.

Thai ginger, known as galangal or laos, appears skinny and fingerlike compared to common ginger. Dried galangal can be found in most Asian markets, and fresh galangal can also be found occasionally. Some say it tastes like a cross between ginger and cardamom. Common ginger can be substituted for galangal.

The hard part about Thai food seems to be getting the special Thai ingredients. With those at hand, you merely need to stir-fry seafood and accompaniments.

Thai Squid Salad

Ingredients for 4 servings:

4 stalks lemon grass, divided
Peanut oil
1 pound squid bodies, cleaned and cut into rings
1 ounce fish sauce
Chopped hot peppers or pepper paste (to taste)
Juice of 2 limes
1 ounce ginger, minced
2 medium red onions, sliced in paper-thin rings
1 large bunch cilantro
1 bunch fresh basil leaves

Chop the tender white parts of the lemon grass into thin slices; chop the tough green parts into 2-inch lengths. Place some peanut oil in a wok and stir-fry the squid rings and green parts of the lemon grass for 30 seconds or so, just until the squid barely cooks.

Remove and discard the green parts of the lemon grass. Set the squid aside to cool to room temperature. Mix the fish sauce, hot peppers, lime juice, the rest of the lemon grass, and minced ginger to make a dressing. Toss the dressing with the remaining ingredients and serve.

Tart Fish Soup

Ingredients for 6 servings:

6 stalks lemon grass
2 red onions
12 thin slices ginger
1 ounce peanut oil
1 quart fish stock
Chopped peppers or paste (to taste)
1 pound prawns, peeled with tails left on
2 pounds whitefish (cod, rockfish) in chunks
1 cup rice vinegar
1 ounce honey
Sprigs of mint and cilantro

Peel and cut the tough parts from the lemon grass. With the flat blade of a large knife, lightly crush the lemon grass. Either grate the onions or puree them in a food processor. Then add the lemon grass, onions, and ginger to the oil in a wok or large skillet and sauté for 5 minutes.

Add the fish stock and peppers and bring to a simmer. Add the shrimp and fish and simmer for 10 minutes. Just before serving, add the vinegar and honey. Garnish with mint and cilantro.

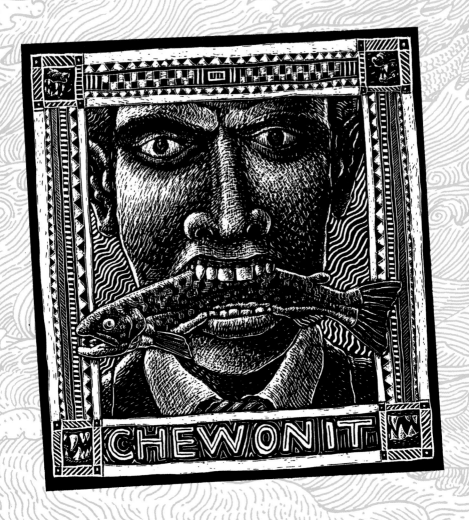

CHEW ON IT

Don't be
intimidated
by sushi...

CHAPTER 33
JAPANESE: EATING IT RAW

What the Japanese brought to the party was the reinvention of how we look at freshness in fish. The quality of fish depends on how you catch it and clean it and handle it. Nowadays, the quality fish marketers say you gut and bleed your fish right after you catch it and then right away you pack it carefully on plenty of ice and keep it ice cold all the way to the market. With that kind of care, you can eat fish raw, and here's how.

Sushi

It takes years of apprenticeships and training to become a sushi chef, but it only takes guts and seaweed to enjoy the amateur versions. Here's a sea vegetarian suggestion. First, the sushi rice. Take 2 cups of real rice (using instant rice is like putting catsup on chateaubriand) and cook according to instructions, except add a chunk of kombu (sugar wrack) during boiling. Meanwhile, mix up 2 ounces of rice vinegar, 2 tablespoons of honey, and 1 tablespoon of mirin (substitute pale, dry sherry).

Place the cooked rice in a nonmetallic bowl and slowly mix in the rice vinegar mixture, stirring constantly while fanning the rice to cool it down faster. Once at room temperature, it's ready.

While waiting, lay out a sheet of toasted nori (store-bought laver; you'll probably not be able to match nori with beach-foraged porphyra) on a heavy cloth napkin. I've even used a paper towel.

Once cooled, place a layer of sushi rice evenly on the nori sheet, leaving a 2-inch margin of nori exposed at only one end. In the center of the rice layer, lay a length of kelp midrib or chunks of pickled bullwhip kelp. To roll the sushi, it helps to have an official sushi mat but you can use a paper towel or napkin as well.

Now, using the roll or napkin to help (but, of course, peeling the napkin back and not rolling it into the rice), roll the nori into a long cylinder, with the exposed 2-inch margin of nori being on the outside. Let the roll sit for 5 minutes, then remove the napkin. With a wetted knife blade of your sharpest thin knife, slice the roll into 1-inch chunks and serve it with soy sauce on the side.

Needless to say, the center portion of sushi can consist of a huge variety of vegetables and seafoods at various stages of life, as well as some of that fantastic green horseradish-like "wasabi" that I consume in great quantities for sinus maintenance. Don't be intimidated by sushi though. You'll appreciate it much more at restaurants if you try it at home or on your boat.

Japanese Baked Fish Omelet

Grind or blend ½ cup of deboned, skinless herring fillets. While slowly blending, add a dozen eggs, one at a time. Then add 1 tablespoon of honey (optional) and 1 ounce of sake. In a large, hot skillet, pour in the egg mixture, allowing the bottom to set, about 4 minutes. Bake at 250°F for 1 hour, or until a knife inserted into the center comes out clean. Run a sharp knife around the edge, place a serving dish on top of the skillet, and flip it over so that the omelet drops into the serving dish. Slice the omelet into 1-inch strips. Serve at room temperature.

Sake-Cooked Herring

Combine a cup of sake with 1 ounce of honey, 1 tablespoon of grated ginger, and 1 tablespoon of soy sauce. Bring to a boil. Drop in 2 pounds of boneless herring fillets and return to a boil, then reduce to low heat. Set a heavy pot lid directly on the fish to keep them intact. Simmer for 30 minutes until the liquid is almost all evaporated. Serve hot or at room temperature. Use the remaining liquid as a sauce.

Teriyaki Herring

Use the sauce as above for a marinade for the herring. After 4 or more hours of soaking, skewer the herring fillets on bamboo slivers and grill over a charcoal hibachi or in the oven over a foil-lined pan. Baste the fish in the marinade while broiling. It should take but 5 minutes or so to cook. Serve on a bed of lettuce.

Japanese Cod Salad

Ingredients for 4 servings:

4 ounces Japanese buckwheat noodles
1 pound fresh cod, in chunks
2 ounces rice vinegar
1 ounce red miso
1 tablespoon freshly grated ginger
6 green onions, cut in 2-inch lengths
Cilantro for garnish

Cook and drain the noodles and fish. Mix the vinegar, miso, and ginger. Toss the mixture with the noodles, onions, and fish, and garnish with cilantro.

A MAN NEEDS A FISH

LIKE A WOMAN NEEDS A BICYCLE

OK, OK!
Just don't
shock me again...

I'll tell.
I'll tell!

CHAPTER 34
SECRETS STOLEN FROM A GREAT ITALIAN RESTAURANT

Once upon a time, Juneau's *Bellezza* was known for the best fresh seafood, done in Tuscany fashion. Now they've relocated to Seattle as *Serafino's*, so that's where we eat in the Lower 48. In Juneau, diners were encouraged to eat in traditional European style in a series of courses. They began with antipasti. They offered oysters, steamed mussels and clams, fried and marinated calamari, and various other delicacies. Salads were served either before (American-style) or after (European-style) the entree. The salads featured extra virgin olive oil, freshly ground cheese, basil, toasted pine nuts, fresh spinach, and the like.

The next course—not to be slighted—was the pasta. Made locally at *La Pasta*, the pasta dishes included linguine, spinach fettuccine, and capellini, among others. Pasta excels with seafood, as evidenced by the salmon with cream sauce over linguini (this recipe and others, pieced together from the tape transcript, will follow). The entrees follow, offering more pasta and a horde of fantastic seafood recipes, specializing in swordfish, mussels, clams, and shrimp (purchased fresh locally). Desserts, *dolci*, were prepared by the baker and presented on a tray.

Follow all of this with coffee and wine. The coffee, a Viennese and French roast blend, prepared and ground daily by *Heritage Northwest*, comes best as espresso or cappuccino. For dessert wine, several sherries and ports are offered.

Clearly, *Bellezza* was a worthy target for my mission. How does one extract closely guarded secrets from professional chefs? Not all restaurant secrets are easy to obtain. Some chefs brag. Some chefs consider their recipes their own proprietary trademarks and hide the ingredients in unmarked bottles. Sometimes getting recipes from restaurants is like industrial espionage: search through the garbage, bribe the busboy, blackmail the owner. After considering all the options, I chose the latest technology.

Q ❚ *What is the secret of Bellezza's cioppino?*

A ❚ It's the oregano. (The KGB-surplus lie detector senses a subtle change in resistance of Chef Tim's skin and automatically sends 15,000 volts through his body. Chef Tim screams. His feet are shackled in a bucket of water for special effect. It takes 20 seconds for the lie detector to restabilize.)

Q ❚ *Come now, oregano is in all cioppino. Once again, the secret of Bellezza's cioppino.*

A ❚ It's . . . it's the saffron. (The truth.)

Q ❚ *Is that ALL?*

A ❚ Yes. (Lie. 20,000 volts this time. The bucket tips. A minute passes.)

Q ❚ *Do you think I like this? Just tell me about the cioppino.*

A ❚ OK, OK! Just don't shock me again. It's the stock. It's the mussels. I'll tell. I'll tell!

And now. . . I am pleased to share the recipes and secrets of Bellezza:

Begin at the beginning: the fish stock. It goes into nearly everything. Bellezza used scraps and bones from swordfish and sturgeon when available. Salmon stock is too rich. Also avoid sole or flounder. Spices were not specified, but the standard-issue Italian additives invariably included garlic, oregano, olive oil, freshly ground pepper, and wine (dry white in this case).

Other basics included garlic and basil. At Bellezza, garlic gloves were pureed with olive oil in a food processor and refrigerated. This way the garlic doesn't dry out and is ready for instant use. Whole cloves were also stored in olive oil, imparting a flavor to the oil and preserving the cloves.

Pesto

Basil, another Italian staple, forms the basis for pesto. Fresh basil is hard to find, but pesto keeps well for weeks in a refrigerator and can be frozen. Take about 2 cups of fresh basil leaves, add ½ cup of good olive oil, 2 garlic cloves and, if available, 1 ounce of pine nuts. Place this in a blender or food processor and mix at high speed. If it is to be frozen, this is as far as you go. To finish pesto, mix in by hand freshly ground Parmesan and Romano cheese, in equal amounts, about 1 part cheese mixture to 4 parts ground basil. Pesto appeared on

Bellezza's menu served on linguini, but it is commonly used with fish and soups.

Marinara Sauce

Another staple was the tomato-based marinara sauce. Chop very finely a large bunch of fresh basil (or about half a batch of pesto) and 6 cloves of garlic (or about an ounce of garlic puree). Add a handful of chopped onion. Place all this in a saucepan and add 2 ounces of olive oil and 2 8-ounce cans of canned plum tomatoes, Progresso brand being the choice at Bellezza, drained and seeds removed. Tomato puree, Progresso brand again, saves the pain of deseeding. Add ½ cup of red wine. Spice with freshly ground white pepper and oregano. Simmer for a long time (6 hours is a long time), stirring each half hour. If it gets too thick, add water or more red wine. This freezes well.

Cioppino

The Bellezza house favorite was Cioppino, an Italian dish straight from San Francisco. A couple secrets here: first, any seafood will do (almost), so long as it's fresh. The name *cioppino* comes from "chip in" as in throwing the catch of seafood into a pot at the end of the day. The favorite fish at Bellezza were sturgeon, snapper, and swordfish, which are steamed on the side to avoid being mashed up in the stew. Likewise, clams are steamed separately to keep the occasional "mud clam" from destroying the whole batch. The clam liquid is saved for the sauce.

Oily fish like salmon and sablefish are to be avoided because they would overpower this dish. The same goes for oysters. Avoid squid, too; this cooking method makes it too tough.

The sauce starts with Italian plum tomato paste mixed with fish stock and spices: oregano, thyme, garlic, and saffron. Saffron, made from the sex organs of the crocus, costs plenty and is Secret No. 2. Use lots. The best I can figure, use about a dollar's worth per person. The sauce simmers for 30 minutes.

Meanwhile, steam clams, mussels, crab, prawns, and fish. Do not remove the shells. Serve the sauce on top of the steamed seafood, artistically arranged. Fresh garlic bread goes alongside. Be sure to place a bowl on the table for discarded shells, and have extra towels on hand. Sometimes it's best to lay plastic over the carpet. Cioppino is half eaten with the fingers and the other half sponged up with bread. Not for the squeamish or wee-mannered folk.

Pasta con Salmone

Following the antipasti in traditional style, serve Pasta con Salmone—linguini tossed with salmon strips (both cold smoked or lox work real well) in a rich cream sauce. A little-known secret is that seafood does a number on pasta. The cream sauce starts by reducing heavy cream with standard fish stock and white wine (or brandy—try each). Add freshly ground white pepper. Add a small hunk of butter. After about 10 minutes, lightly toss the bubbling sauce with slivers of salmon, 15 seconds for smoked salmon, a bit longer for uncooked salmon. Serve over *al dente* linguini, garnish with grated Parmesan cheese and caviar, if you have it.

Mussels Puttanesca

CARDSHARKS

Another favorite menu item was Mussels Puttanesca, known in the kitchen as mussels with harlot sauce. There's a story behind this, which I cannot tell all of, but it has to do with being in a hurry. The sauce contains freshly ground white pepper, garlic puree, tomato paste, anchovies, chopped onion, lemon juice, red chile pepper, capers, and chopped black olives. Simmer for at least a half-hour, for a long as 6 hours. It's rich, red, and full of life. Sitting on a mound of capellini and surrounded by steamed mussels, this plucky sauce looks downright feisty, ready for all comers.

Linguini con Vongole

More pasta and seafood on Bellezza's menu included fresh clams in a sauce of cream, white wine, olive oil, and butter, topped with Parmesan cheese, served over linguini. The cream sauce goes like this: to 4 ounces of heavy cream, add 1 ounce of white wine, 1 ounce of olive oil, 1 teaspoon of garlic puree, and a few drops of lemon juice. Notice how the subtlety of spices in a cream sauce compares with the rich tomato-based sauces. Add 4 ounces of chopped steamed clams and the juices. Reduce by simmering for 10 minutes. Toss linguini with soft butter, add the clam sauce, and garnish with grated Parmesan cheese.

Grilling

Grilled fish rates high, because of fast cooking, high moisture retention (done properly), easy adaptation to sauces, and its Adriatic origins. Use a super-hot grill, cooking the fish until the grill scores a brownish-black mark on the bottom of the fish. Only then does the fish have enough firmness to easily flip over. Both salmon and halibut grill well. For salmon fillets, a cream-and-fennel sauce is topped by cucumber. Start with the reliable fish stock, add cream and fennel, and reduce. Continue to make up with more stock. Carefully add Pernod, tasting as you go—don't overdo it. Serve with cucumber slices on top.

Frittatas

Frittata is Italy's answer to quiche. Almost any seafood and any fresh produce can be combined. Frittatas are slowly cooked in a heavy skillet, often on top of a stove. But a frittata must be cooked on both sides. If you have an oven, simply place a nearly cooked frittata under the broiler for a minute or so to finish it off. A more adventurous method would be to flip it in the skillet like a pancake. Then there's the two-skillet technique, rotating the frittata into a second skillet acting as a lid.

Anyhow, for 4 persons, use a half-dozen eggs, beaten up with grated Parmesan or mozzarella cheese. Add ingredients. If slow-cooking vegetables like onion, green peppers, zucchini, asparagus, and so forth are to be used, sauté them lightly first and allow them to cool before adding them to the beaten egg mixture. Fresh spinach, Italian tomatoes, chard, and the like also are recommended. Chopped fresh basil (or pesto) should be added. Seafood options include shrimp, scallops, salmon, and crab.

Mix all the ingredients well and cook slowly on medium heat until 90 percent of the mixture has set. Add a glob of marinara sauce and a handful of grated Parmesan cheese, and place under the broiler until the cheese is melted and it's fully firm. Cut into pie-like wedges and serve hot.

At Bellezza, they've invented a method to cook frittata quickly by reserving and later folding in egg whites, but that's a secret I didn't pick up. The slow version works fine at home. Another great idea for the Sunday brunch, served with champagne. And easily cooked on board your boat. No oven needed, just that heavy cast-iron skillet over low heat.

Marinated Calamari

For antipasti, the marinated calamari has always been a favorite of mine. For this, Tim has two major secrets. First, the celery, leeks, and red peppers must be diced very finely. Not food-processed, but diced by hand, very, very finely. Second, the squid must be cooked with very hot oil. Expect smoke and fumes; the squid should "blast off." Large squid should be cut in thin strips. Small squid should be cut in rings. Save the tentacles for something else—chopped and stuffed or in soups or stock. The marinade is 1 part olive oil to 1 part vegetable oil to 1 part red wine. Add oregano and basil. Marinate the sautéed squid and vegetables overnight in the refrigerator. Serve it on a bed of romaine, garnished with chopped green onions and freshly grated cheese.

Halibut in Garlic Sauce

For halibut, garlic sauce does the trick. First, rub the halibut with the olive oil from the bottle of garlic cloves. Grill it as described earlier. Make garlic sauce by mixing 4 parts white wine with 2 parts lemon juice and 1 part garlic puree. Place in a saucepan and add fresh parsley and 2 parts butter and heat until the butter bubbles. Serve while the garlic sauce is hot.

The rest of Bellezza's menu contained veal and chicken specialties. The Pollo Tommaso—boneless breast of chicken topped with proscuitto and mozzarella in a marsala sauce—will remain a secret no matter how many volts are applied. The famous meat sauce à la Bolognese takes days to prepare, also to remain undisclosed.

Somehow, Bellezza seemed unthreatened by these revelations. We can only try out imitations and compare them with the real thing. The idea is sound: fresh seafood, handled and cooked with quality. Light, subtle cream sauces and rich, hearty tomato sauces. Combined with good wines, homemade pasta, and a fine atmosphere, Bellezza was where you'd want your seafood to end up. That's no secret.

CHAPTER 35

ITALIAN: PASTA AND SEAFOOD– A GREAT COMBO

Forget everything you have ever learned about pasta. It is either wrong, or it doesn't apply to seafood pasta dishes. And don't believe the experts when they tell you pasta is simple to cook; a dozen things can go awry when cooking pasta. Nevertheless, once the basic techniques have been learned and proper sauces prepared, pasta complements seafood dishes with simple satisfaction.

Pasta suits the mariner's eating style as well. Pasta stores easily without refrigeration, cooks quickly with few utensils, and provides the right kind of energy for offshore demands. Note that marathon runners and football players now "carb up" by eating pasta prior to strenuous physical events. Pasta, properly chosen, provides fiber and nutrition, as well as energy. And properly sauced, it does not cause you to gain weight.

Proper selection of pasta can be easy up to a point. To begin with, ignore any pasta not made with durum or semolina. Dry pasta can be as good as or better than fresh pasta. Look for a buff color, not gray, with a dull, finely pitted surface. Specks in the surface may be a good sign. Most experts recommend imported pasta. For seafood, select the long, thin pastas—spaghetti, spaghettini, linguine, and so forth.

On cooking pasta, experts agree on some things and differ on others. All agree to use large amounts of water, at least a gallon per pound of dry pasta. They also agree that the water should be in a rapid, if not passionate, boil before adding the pasta. They all describe the crunchiness of properly cooked pasta as *al dente* ("to the tooth") and denounce mushy pasta caused by overcooking. They insist that hot pasta meals must be served instantly and on preheated plates.

But the experts also differ, sometimes with explanations and sometimes without. Some add olive oil to the boiling water to prevent pasta from sticking together. Others add olive oil to prevent the foam from boiling over. Others admonish against oil. Most add salt to boiling water, but others say it can be omitted. Many say to add pasta to boiling water all at once; others say to add it in small batches. Some experts use colanders to drain the water; others lift the pasta out with forks.

The hardest part of cooking pasta is knowing when to stop. Ignore any instructions on the box. Test the pasta each minute or two during cooking. Lift some out, let it cool briefly, then bite it. Stop cooking well before the pasta loses its crunchiness. Remember that pasta will continue to cook in non-boiling water. Quickly remove the pasta from the hot water and place it in a warm bowl containing a tablespoon of olive oil. Toss the pasta only briefly with the oil. Save the hot water in case you have undercooked or overdrained the pasta, or for use in sauces.

Be prepared to serve cooked pasta within seconds. Have the table set, the sauces cooked, wines opened, serving plates and eating dishes in a warm oven, and guests seated with the gum out of their mouths. Toss the pasta quickly with the sauce, serve on prewarmed plates, and avoid delays of frills, ceremony, manners, and garnishes.

So much for traditional pasta cooking. For the seafood sauces, modify the traditional method by deliberately undercooking the pasta by at least a minute or two. Set the undercooked pasta in the prewarmed, oiled bowl. Meanwhile, you will have been preparing the sauce and seafood. During the last minute of cooking the seafood, add the undercooked pasta and simmer for the final minute. As before, serve immediately.

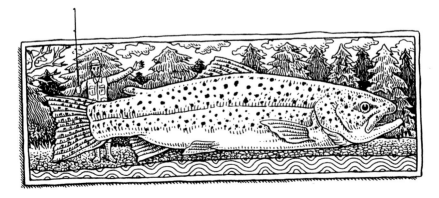

Batutto Snapper with Linguine

Batutto means the sautéed vegetables that form the basic sauce stock. Herbs can be fresh basil, as below, or fresh oregano or mint. Such recipes always call for cayenne pepper over black pepper. With snapper or other white fish, the cayenne adds a zing that you will appreciate. For more zing, add red pepper flakes as well.

Ingredients for 4 servings:
3 cloves garlic, smashed and chopped
1 onion, chopped
1 stalk celery, sliced thinly
1 carrot, in thin peelings
1 tablespoon olive oil
1 teaspoon or more red cayenne pepper
1 cup white wine
1 pound snapper fillets, in 1-inch chunks
1 pound dry linguine
1 small bunch basil

Start by using a large skillet to lightly sauté the garlic, onion, celery, and carrot in the olive oil. When these vegetables are barely softened, add the cayenne and wine. Simmer until reduced in volume by about half, maybe 15 minutes. Then lay the snapper chunks atop the vegetables and cover the skillet.

About the time you have added the wine to the sauce, start the pasta water boiling, at least a gallon on the hottest burner in a large pot. Use seawater if available. Add a dollop of pesto for oil and flavor. Place a serving bowl and table dishes in a warm oven.

Once the water has begun a passionate boil, add the pasta all at once, stirring to make sure it does not stick together. Test the pasta frequently and remove it to the warm, oiled serving bowl in an undercooked state.

After 10 minutes of steaming the fish, remove the cover and test it. If it flakes easily and looks done, add the chopped basil and pasta. Gently toss together and let simmer for another minute. Serve immediately.

Summer Seafood Pasta Salad

For pasta lovers, tomatoes mean the Italian plum variety. If you cannot find fresh plum tomatoes, they take to the can very well.

Ingredients for 4 servings:

8 ounces dry pasta
1 ounce olive oil
Juice of a lemon
4 plum tomatoes, chopped
1 16-ounce can of salmon, flaked
1 bunch fresh basil leaves, chopped

Poached fish would better replace canned; and fresh spinach can replace the basil.

Cook the pasta as always. Drain, but don't be in a hurry to serve. Toss with the olive oil, then with the lemon juice, then with the remaining ingredients.

Turmeric Prawns

Ingredients for 4 servings:

4 ounces dry linguine
1 cup fish stock
2 tablespoons turmeric, divided
3 cloves garlic, chopped finely
2 ounces olive oil
1 pound prawns, peeled, tails intact
4 carrots, sliced into thin strips
1 cup snow peas
6 green onions, cut in 3-inch lengths
4 ounces dry white wine

Boil the linguine in plenty of water with the fish stock and half the turmeric. While that cooks, sauté the garlic in the oil, then add the prawns and sauté for a minute or so. Remove the prawns.

Sauté the carrots, snow peas, and green onions for a minute or two. Add the wine and remaining turmeric and boil for a few minutes, adding the prawns and drained linguine just before serving. Simmer long enough to assure the prawns are cooked through, and serve on hot plates.

Scallops Pancetta

Scallops shine in the company of bacon, in this case, a cured Italian type, pancetta. Substitute slab bacon, with the rind removed, chopped into ¼-inch pieces. Be generous with the hot pepper.

Ingredients for 4 servings:

8 ounces spaghettini
4 ounces pancetta, chopped in thick slivers
2 ounces olive oil
4 cloves garlic, minced
1 large red onion, sliced in rings
1 pound scallops
1 pound snow peas
4 ounces Greek olives
4 ounces parsley sprigs
4 ounces freshly grated Parmesan cheese
Hot red pepper flakes to taste

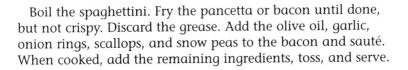

Boil the spaghettini. Fry the pancetta or bacon until done, but not crispy. Discard the grease. Add the olive oil, garlic, onion rings, scallops, and snow peas to the bacon and sauté. When cooked, add the remaining ingredients, toss, and serve.

Smoked Cod and Scotch

Ingredients for 4 servings:

12 ounces dry spaghetti
4 ounces heavy cream
1 pound smoked cod or sablefish, flaked
1 jigger Scotch whiskey
Parsley for garnish
Parmesan cheese for garnish

Cook and drain the pasta as always. Heat the cream, add the flaked cod and whiskey. Toss the pasta with the fish mixture and serve on hot plates. Garnish with sprigs of parsley and freshly grated Parmesan cheese.

GRANNIE'S GONE BUT THE COFFEE'S ON

CHAPTER 36

A SPOT OF OHIO:
GRANDMA SHRIVER'S FANTASTIC FISH-AND-ONION HOT POTATO SALAD

Grandma Shriver isn't with us anymore, but her fantastic fish recipe thrives on. Onion lovers rejoice because onions can glorify, dominate, or simply take part in this Old World fare. And if you leave out the fish, you have one wunderbar German hot potato salad. I like to serve this on my boat because it's easy, fast, feeds a big unruly crew, and uses only one pot. If you have Scandinavians aboard, you can serve it for breakfast. Later in the day, serve it with beer.

Start by soaking chopped raw onions in vinegar. Boil some quartered potatoes along with some sort of fish. I like bottomfish, especially rockfish or cod, but go ahead and use expensive fish if you must. When the potatoes are easily stabbed, separate them out, add butter, and mash them. Mix in the drained onions and flaked fish. That's it. I told you it was easy.

Now if you want potato salad, leave out the fish. The basic onions and potatoes work fine for simple folks, but you can fancify it by adding crisp bacon, parsley, boiled eggs, chopped pickles, mustard, mayonnaise, spices, and so on.

The secrets basically lie with the onions. The longer they soak the better. The colder they are the better. Try various types, amounts, and mixes of onions. The red ones look great. So do the green ones. True aficionados marinate the fish in vinegar along with the onions. And notice I've not mentioned any spices to compete with the onions—this is their moment of stardom.

If you want to get real fancy and don't mind potato under your fingernails, make fish balls. Squeeze the mix into balls, dip them in egg and batter, and deep-fat-fry them. And with Scandinavians around for breakfast, add poached eggs to the crater in a mound of the hot potato mix.

Grandma Shriver could have left me money, but that would have been taxed, foolishly spent, and forgotten. Much better to remember her when I fix her Fantastic Fish-and-Onion Hot Potato Salad. She told me to keep it a secret until the world was ready for it. She wants you to try it now.

BASSA NOVA

INDEX

INDEX

About the Author

When Randy Bayliss isn't helping diners with their menu selections, you'll find him cruising Alaska's Inside Passage or scavenging the beach for edibles. In his other (paying) life, Bayliss is an environmental consultant who splits his time between Juneau, Alaska, and New Mexico, and specializes in hazardous waste cleanups. No reflection on his kitchen. Bayliss has been published in *Alaska* magazine, *National Fisherman*, *Alaska Fisherman's Journal*, and *Sea Kayaker*.

THE LUMPSUCKER VISITATION

About the Artist

The marriage of Ray Troll's fish-o-centric art with a seafood cookbook is no accident. Troll and Bayliss are longtime friends and first-time collaborators. Troll lives and works in Ketchikan, Alaska, but his travels and fabulous art are far-reaching. You'll find his work in prints, T-shirts, aprons, posters, cards, murals, magazines, and in prestigious museums as traveling exhibits. Other books include *Sharkabet: A Sea of Sharks from A to Z*, *Shocking Fish Tales*, *Planet Ocean*, and *Raptors, Fossils, Fins and Fangs*. To see more of Ray Troll's imaginative artwork, browse www.trollart.com.